Nicaragua

First published in 1986, *Nicaragua*, written from an insider's point of view breaks the barrier of disinformation which has surrounded the Sandinista revolution. To accomplish this task the author discusses the major forces that have shaped Nicaragua's development during the past decade as well as all pertinent events leading to and following the revolution. It is the author's contention that the Sandinista revolution is an unusual combination of armed struggle to reach power and democratic procedures to build a new society. This makes the revolution a very dangerous example for the stability of a hegemonic state that tries to pacify the needs of the masses by means of repression and spurious applications of democratic principles. This book's main thesis is that socialism and democracy are not contradictory but are part of the same process. Thus, any attempt to think in terms of necessary stages is misreading the classics of Marx and Lenin.

This book will be of interest to scholars and researchers of political science, Latin American studies, Latin American history, and politics.

Nicaragua

Revolution and Democracy

José Luis Coraggio

Routledge
Taylor & Francis Group

First published in 1986
by Allen & Unwin Ltd.

This edition first published in 2024 by Routledge
4 Park Square, Milton Park, Abingdon, Oxon, OX14 4RN

and by Routledge
605 Third Avenue, New York, NY 10017

Routledge is an imprint of the Taylor & Francis Group, an informa business

Publisher's Note
The publisher has gone to great lengths to ensure the quality of this reprint but points
out that some imperfections in the original copies may be apparent.

Disclaimer
The publisher has made every effort to trace copyright holders and welcomes
correspondence from those they have been unable to contact.

A Library of Congress record exists under ISBN: 0044970196

ISBN: 978-1-032-78356-7 (hbk)
ISBN: 978-1-003-48750-0 (ebk)
ISBN: 978-1-032-78357-4 (pbk)

Book DOI 10.4324/9781003487500

NICARAGUA
Revolution and Democracy

José Luis Coraggio

Coordinadora Regional de Investigaciones Econòmicas y Sociales
Managua, Nicaragua

Boston
Allen & Unwin, Inc.
London   Sydney

This work was originally published in Spanish under the title:
Nicaragua: Revolución y Democracia

© 1985 by Editorial Linea S.A. de C.V., Mexico City, Mexico

English edition copyright © 1986 by Allen & Unwin, Inc.

Allen & Unwin, Inc.
8 Winchester Place
Winchester, MA 01890, USA

George Allen & Unwin (Publishers), Ltd.
40 Museum Street, London, WC1A LU, UK

George Allen & Unwin (Publishers), Ltd.
Park Lane, Hemel Hempstead, Herts HP2 4TE, UK

George Allen & Unwin Australia Pty Ltd.
8 Napier Street, North Sydney, NSW 2060, Australia

Library of Congress Cataloging-in-Publication Data
Coraggio, José Luis.
  Nicaragua, revolution and democracy.

  Translation of: Nicaragua, revolución y democracia.
  Bibliography: p.
  Includes index.
  1. Nicaragua—Politics and government—1979–   . I. Title.
F1528.C66713   1986   972.85′053   86–17362
ISBN 0–04–497019–6 (pbk. : alk. paper)

British Library Cataloguing in Publication Data
Coraggio, José Luis.
  Nicaragua: revolution and democracy.
  1. Revolutions—Nicaragua   2. Nicaragua
  —Politics and government—1979–
  I. Title
  322.4′2′097285   JL1602
ISBN 0–04–497019–6

MANUFACTURED IN THE UNITED STATES OF AMERICA

Contents

Preface to the English Edition

Except for minor changes made in the original Spanish version, this book was basically finished in December 1984. Since then, more than a year has passed, and events in Nicaragua have continued to develop very rapidly. In my opinion, the main events that have taken place confirm the principal theses presented here regarding the profoundly democratic nature of the Sandinista People's Revolution. Below I will discuss some of these events.

The revolutionary government's decision to deal a strategic blow to the counterrevolution during 1985, sure that the Reagan administration's goal was to prolong the war of attrition, led to calling up thousands of young men to the Patriotic Military Service. This was used by the more recalcitrant opposition as an issue, trying to exacerbate the population's natural reluctance to participate in an army certain to confront forces armed by the world's foremost power. However, the draft was carried out, and in early 1986 the first contingents of draftees were discharged, and they have returned to the schools and workplaces with a clear idea of what the counterrevolution is: They have suffered ambushes orchestrated out of neighboring countries; they have seen peasants who have been tortured and mutilated and whose daughters have been raped, but above all they have seen that the Contras have already become demoralized by their own corruption and their inability to reach the goals laid out by the agencies financing them. At the same time, the Sandinista People's Army and the revolutionary government made notable advances in redefining the relationship between economic policies, ideological struggle, and military struggle, establishing a more organic relationship with the civilian population in the zones affected by counterrevolutionary activity.

A major factor contributing to this was the change in the Frente Sandinista de Liberación Nacional (FSLN—Sandinista National Liberation Front) cadre assignments to areas where the state and the revolutionary party had had only a weak presence, which had sometimes resulted in a perception of a power vacuum and of unresponsiveness due to the lack of contact with the peasant bases in these areas.

Simultaneously, the policy of assigning supplies began little by little to benefit the country's outlying areas at the expense of the bloated and increasingly unproductive city of Managua. Also, it was realized that relative pricing had hurt the food-producing peasantry, and this also was corrected. The economic situation of the majorities had been deteriorating, due to the war and the persistent lack of development that were impossible to resolve through political will. At the same time, concealed by the anarchy resulting from disorganization in the formal markets, certain groups of intermediaries had gotten rich, involving a growing mass of hoarder middlemen in their network throughout the country.

This critical situation showed the government the errors it had made in economic management. A program of macroeconomic measures—for which the need had been foreseen in 1983 and that had begun to be applied before the elections, when subsidies on the main consumer goods were reduced—had a strong impact in February 1985, setting off an inflation rate that by the end of the year was reaching 300 percent annually. Defense spending, an inevitable response to the foreign aggression, had reached 50 percent of the national budget; this, together with the continued deterioration of the terms of trade and the effects of the war on production, increased the scarcity of goods and the deterioration of the productive apparatus and the infrastructure. The advances made in social spending also had to be cut back. Successive wage hikes (between 20 and 100 percent each) tried to win the war between prices and salaries in favor of the working classes, and the state and the mass organizations began to ready their forces to confront the problems of speculation and the black market as efficiently as possible.

The policy of encouraging the production of exportable goods was continued, by which private Nicaraguan producers could earn profits (basically in cordobas but with additional incentives in dollars) for exporting goods that in other countries of the region were causing bankruptcies (i.e., the case of cotton production).

However, economic harassment—the blocking of financing by multilateral credit agencies, the elimination of the sugar quota, the trade embargo decreed in March 1985—adopted by the U.S. administration, comparable to similar measures taken against the Allende government in Chile, in violation of international and even U.S. law, would further aggravate the difficult situation. The result of undertaking to create and maintain a mixed economy and pluralism in the context of a war economy and the growing foreign strangulation—aggravated by the economic harassment by a country that had previously been its main supplier and market for its goods—was growing inflation, a tendency to favor individual economic survival over community-oriented tasks, and a reduction in participation in mass organizations. Within the state, the term *accumulation model* for transition was abandoned in favor of *survival model* for the resistance.

If the Reagan administration's goal was to destabilize the government by appealing to popular discontent, it would be hard to find more favorable conditions than those it achieved in 1985: the pressure of the military draft, growing state controls in order to avoid speculation in the context of an increasingly difficult situation for the masses, at the same time as the capitalist sectors continued to enjoy their privileges of high incomes and even access to consumer goods considered to be luxuries in Latin America's third poorest country (the importation of cars to be sold in dollars was permitted as a way of absorbing some of the dollars that had been given as economic incentives for production, etc.). Finally, the popular sectors that had been able to regain a comfortable position through speculation saw themselves under attack for sabotaging production—production was the condition for making military defense possible.

However, despite all this, the revolution continued to deepen its democratic nature. As regards democratic mechanisms, the institutionalization of the new political system continued as planned. Following what are considered by numerous international observers (such as the Latin American Studies Association) to be exceptionally clean elections, the National Assembly was formed including all the parties that had participated in the elections; it began the task of writing a new constitution for the country. As a result of this effort, in February 1986, during the anniversary of General Augusto Cesar Sandino's assassination, the material elaborated by the multipartisan commission charged with writing the constitution was presented, including a group of points that presented dissenting positions and a group of specific proposals made by individual parties. This material will be discussed in open forums that will include participation by all parties and popular sectors and will then return to the commission where the final draft will be written. What has come out of the consensus up to this point shows the elements of a republican system, with the division of the state into separate branches, subject to direct elections, through universal and secret balloting, of the national executive branch and the legislative representatives. As a member of the international community, Nicaragua is unconditionally committed to human and social rights (the United States has not signed the United Nations' Convention on Human Rights). Within a spirit that we could call *liberal*, the political philosophy underlying the project is implemented in a presidential type of political regime.

During the process of drafting the constitution, some parties tried to discredit the process itself, withdrawing from the assembly when they could not impose their position; but they finally had to return when the FSLN did not accept the blackmail implied by these threats. The FSLN itself had to change the way it dealt with relations in the assembly and learned to listen to the opposition and take its points of view into account, while also overcoming the temptation to use its majority position to "bulldoze" (a practice that scandalizes no one in the English Parliament). As regards the formation of a substantive democracy, a drastic change was made as regards agrarian reform that had originally been more oriented toward state and cooperative development and that turned over massive amounts of individual property to peasants without land, or with little land. By the end of 1985, symbols were mixed with the reality of a true popular revolution during land title ceremonies as each peasant was given his deed and a rifle to defend the land just given to him. The population was called on to join the reserves, and their response was massive: The people prepared themselves to increase the costs of an eventual, direct U.S. invasion, the probability of which increased with the disbanding of the counterrevolutionary forces. Toward October of that same year, assemblies were held at the base levels of the Sandinista Defense Committees (CDS), the Sandinista union organizations, and the Luisa Amanda Espinoza Nicaraguan Women's Association. In all three cases, blasting criticisms were made of bureaucracy, not only within the state but also in the leadership of the organizations themselves. The FSLN set out to work more actively with the bases and, as had been agreed to in 1984, possibilities were opened up for political competition within the CDSs as the nonpartisan community organizations began to elect their leaders by secret ballot as a prelude to the coming municipal elections.

While the FSLN thus deepened the process of developing the people as the revolution's subject, some political parties—left behind by the momentum of the popular movement and with no other arguments than their history of opposing Somocism—resorted to blackmail. Some, such as a top leader of the Independent Liberal party, even went so far as to say that they would sit back and watch the conflict between the Reagan administration and a "totalitarian" project they did not support, insisting on a self-isolating line that was in line with Reagan's position but that was historically self-destructive. On the other hand, parties such as the Conservative Democratic party or the Popular Social Christian party threw themselves into an open political competition, trying to win new bases and help guide the revolution according to their own programs. With certain reservations, the Marxist Left supported the FSLN; however, they considered it too bourgeois due to its maintenance of an alliance with the bourgeoisie and its failure to put into practice the typical program of nationalization and workers' control over production that they supported.

The FSLN dealt with the Miskito question, which was broadened to include the question of all the minorities of the Atlantic coast, with new and determined approaches. Several general amnesties were decreed for the Miskitos who had taken up arms, and they were invited to return to their former communities. Negotiations were started with the armed faction not directly under the CIA's orders; this group was led by Brooklyn Rivera who was invited to come into the country, which he did several times. In fact, following these negotiations, a suspension of hostilities was reached with local indigenous leaders who were not disarmed. A consultation was begun at the community level about the Autonomy Project for the Atlantic coast. If, in 1985, the international systems of information had not been so intent on hiding or lying about what was happening in Nicaragua, the world would have been surprised: Once again, Nicaragua was making innovations by opening the way to granting autonomy to the ethnic communities with respect for their forms of self-government and economic organization as well as control over their natural resources, on the condition that this not undermine national territorial integrity. Countless Latin American indigenous peoples have fought unsuccessfully against bourgeois governments for a formula like this. The FSLN has proposed that the Autonomy Project be made into a national law and its principles included in the constitution. Also in February 1985, the Moravian church demanded that the U.S. government end its aid to the Contras.

In these months, the "true opposition," as elected by Reagan, was showing its true colors. Not only did the Ramiro Sacasa Democratic Coordinating Board's presidential candidate, Arturo Cruz, go to Honduras to praise the ex-Somoza guards as the defenders of freedom and the only hope for democracy in Nicaragua, but the highest member of the Catholic church hierarchy said a mass for the Contras in Miami at the same time as it continued to refuse to pray for those who had died in Nicaragua while defending their homeland. Later, they unashamedly appeared in Washington in February 1986 at the side of Contra leaders, supporting their requests for aid from the U.S. Congress. Curiously, the Coordinadora and some bishops alike had previously offered to act as "impartial mediators" for what Reagan put forth as the only acceptable action for the FSLN to take: that it sit down to negotiate with the ex-members of National Guard in a so-called "dialogue of national reconciliation." At the same time, Reagan openly declared that his goal was to overthrow the Sandinista government—a rather ambiguous way of defending democracy and the principles of self-determination that the international community has set forth as the rule for peaceful coexistence between peoples. Moreover, these elements never criticized the United States for unilaterally pulling out of the negotiations with the Nicaraguan government held in Manzanillo that had been promoted by the Contadora Group.

In the area of international solidarity, Nicaragua continues to find that its cause is favorably received by Third World countries willing to defy the empire's wrath and mistreatment, especially the efforts made by the Contadora Group and its support group, which in February 1986 clearly stated to the Reagan administration that it should end its aid to the Contras as a way of contributing to peace in the region and allowing for a negotiated solution to the Central American conflict. Thus Nicaragua continues to diversify its international relations—while its leaders travel to Moscow, they also go to every important capital in Western Europe, the Third World, and especially Latin America. They are received with expressions of massive popular support because they are considered to be true defenders of freedom, confronting an unjust war by the very country that should act as the foremost democracy of the Americas.

At the same time, elections have taken place in other Central American countries and the newly elected presidents are attempting to distance themselves from a U.S. policy that appears to be politically out of internal and international control and blinded by its sole objective: to finish off the Sandinista Revolution, now elevated to the rank of a threat to U.S. national security and a danger to humanity!

Having responded by deepening political and social democratization and maintaining its project of national unity, the FSLN has once again shown the world that arrogance and the "big stick" will not prosper; that the revolutions taking place in the capitalist periphery in the name of economic and political democratization for their peoples cannot be overcome; and that the only way to stop their proliferation is a profound transformation of the international economic and political order, from which all peoples can only benefit, including—as protagonists—the North American people themselves.

José Luis Coraggio
Managua
March 1986

xiii

Preface to the Original Edition

At a critical moment in time for the Sandinista People's Revolution, as the people redouble their defense against the constant counterrevolutionary attacks coming from Honduras and from Costa Rican territory, in the face of the obvious threat of a direct military invasion by U.S. troops, with a critical internal economic crisis resulting from the world crisis and the economic boycott orchestrated by the Reagan administration, it is necessary that Latin America realize that the conflict that pairs off a small Central American country against the hegemonic power of the Western hemisphere is not just a question concerning Nicaraguans or even only Central Americans.

The countries belonging to the Contadora Group have taken an active role in finding a political solution to the Central American conflict, trying to check the militarist alternative advocated by the U.S. administration. They are conscious that the alternative posed would have very different consequences for their own future situation. This question has already taken on an "American" (i.e., continental) dimension in that its resolution will color the relationship between the United States and Latin America for decades. This is not so much because it would be the straw that broke the proverbial camel's back of U.S. interventions in detriment to the sovereignty of other countries in the region but rather due to the very nature of the revolutionary process it is trying to drown.

This book will attempt to contribute to some degree to breaking the barrier of disinformation about the Nicaraguan revolution. It tries to reflect a Latin American perspective on a process that has to do with us, not only because it opens up concrete hopes that liberation is possible—no matter how powerful the forces of oppression may be—at the same time as opening up the possibility of a new way of thinking about democracy and socialism that is neither speculative nor based on false consciousness and that does not go back neither to the "good old days" nor to the old manuals.

This book consists of four essays: "Nicaragua, or the Legitimacy of Social Revolution in Latin America," an expanded version of an article published in *Pensamiento Propio* 1, 13 (April 1984); "Democracy and Revolution in Nicaragua," originally published in *Cuadernos de Pensamiento Propio*, Essay Series 7 (May 1984); "Social Movements and Revolution: The Case of Nicaragua," a revised version of a lecture given at the CEDLA Seminar on Latin American Social Movements (Amsterdam, October 1983), and "1984: Elections in Revolution" (an unpublished essay). All these were the result of broader research carried out at the Coordinadora Regional de Investigaciones Económicas y Sociales (CRIES—Regional Coordinating Board of Economic and Social Investigation), headed by Xabier Gorostiaga, whose support I gratefully acknowledge. The Simon Guggenheim Foundation provided a donation so that I could have the time needed to write the two principal works presented here. Rosa María Torres, "compañera" and critic, encouraged my work and, through her own work about popular education in Nicaragua, stimulated the need for emphasizing this revolution's profoundly democratic and creative character.

J.L.C.
Managua
December 1984

Chapter 1

Nicaragua, or the Legitimacy of Social Revolution in Latin America

The Starting Point

In 1979, Nicaragua reappeared in force on the Latin American political and ideological scene. But there were important precedents for the presence of the Nicaraguan people there, which can be found in the Latin American struggle for self-determination. In January 1933, General Sandino's "Crazy Little Army" expelled the U.S. troops who had occupied their country since 1926—the third U.S. occupation. In February 1934, the Latin American peoples mobilized upon hearing the news of Sandino's assassination ordered by Anastasio Somoza, commander of the National Guard that the U.S. Marines organized before withdrawing. In 1961, the Frente Sandinista de Liberación Nacional (FSLN—Sandinista National Liberation Front) was born and began a prolonged struggle against the Somoza dynasty. The sons of Sandino would finish off the government led by Anastasio Somoza García's sons, thus putting an end to the family regime about which Franklin Delano Roosevelt once said: "Somoza is a son of a bitch, but he's our son of a bitch." Thus the "backyard" law enforced so stubbornly by successive U.S. governments lost its main agent in Central America.

On July 19, 1979, the Sandinista People's Revolution triumphed after the FSLN called the people to insurrection in May of that same year. Once again in Latin America, the path of armed struggle combined with the general mobilization of the people was

1

able to overthrow the despotic power of a U.S.-supported dictatorship. Latin America, drained by bloody military dictatorships when not held in check by constant coups, bled by an international economic system that, far from allowing any possible development, confronted the working and peasant masses with even more horrible sacrifices against their humanity, saw this victory with hope. Soon questions would arise as to what type of revolution was taking place in Nicaragua. The world misinformation system rapidly drew a careful curtain, not of silence but of noise, announcing a "new communist dictatorship" threatening the peace of the hemisphere.

However, in these almost six years of revolution, the curtain of misinformation that the U.S. administration has so carefully closed with dedication and uncommon resources could not prevent news from filtering out every so often that something novel was happening in this part of the world. Here was a revolution trying to synthesize Christianity and revolution, in spite of the church hierarchy's violent opposition. Here was a revolution that posed the possibility of a mixed economy, where state-owned enterprises, the peasants—whether individual or cooperative member—and the patriotic bourgeoisie joined together to take the country out of backwardness in spite of the ultra-Left's opposition. This was a revolution that intended to break with the apparent contradiction between political pluralism and social revolution that governed according to laws and that called for the first democratic elections in the history of the country, in spite of the bloody opposition of the principal commander of democracy in the continent. This is a revolution that today harvests its coffee and cotton with a rifle on its shoulder, defending itself against the counterrevolution armed by the Reagan administration and prepared to confront the possibility of a direct intervention by the hemisphere's most powerful military force that has made the overthrow of Sandinism a condition for its international credibility.

This revolution's structural starting point is not very different from the present situation facing other Latin American peoples: economic backwardness, foreign dependence of an agro-export economy that exports raw materials and "dessert" products (cotton, meat, coffee, sugar, bananas) without any industry other than

2

that artificially created by the Central American Common Market dominated by U.S. capital, with obsolete machinery mainly dedicated to putting the "final touch" on agricultural and industrial supplies or imported parts. The relative competitiveness of its agricultural exports is based on the overexploitation of rural workers and the majority of the peasantry that has been marginalized to the worst land, small plots and loaned land, forced into subsistence farming and malnutrition, and pressured to sell its small surplus of basic grains and its labor power for the coffee and cotton harvests. This economy is also characterized by the absence of an industrial proletariat conforming to the models presupposed by the revolutionary theories of the last century. A "marginalized," or informal, population also predominates, especially in Managua, the capital, where almost thirty percent of the nation's population is concentrated. With few exceptions, the feeble bourgeoisie was more oriented to luxury spending than accumulation and was influenced more by the (United) "States" than by the national market or national values. The revolution inherited a backward state, which was a tool of the Somoza family, a transparent screen for a dictatorship that did not need to maintain democratic forms. Economically and demographically, this is a small country that even lacks a census to determine if its population is 3 or 3.5 million but whose obvious majority consists of adolescents and children.

The political revolution—carried out by peasants, marginalized city dwellers and students led by the Sandinista National Liberation Front, synthesizing the national ideology of Sandino's actions and revolutionary theories and incorporating a profound Christian content into its practice—dragged behind it practically all the social sectors who saw the possibility of ending the dictatorship during its final phase.

Revolutionary Nicaragua, located in the center of America between the United States and Latin America, today condenses all of the contradictions that are particular to the peoples of Latin America. It directly confronts the imperialist formula proposed by the U.S. administration for all our peoples, and in so doing, poses the need to redefine inter-American relations and proposes solutions to the despairing situation of the impoverished masses that are oppressed by the dictatorship of the market and of arms.

3

Through its practice, the Sandinista People's Revolution has refreshed the field of democracy and also the camp of socialism, and its contribution goes beyond national boundaries. Nicaragua received an award in 1980 from UNESCO for its National Literacy Campaign; in 1980, Nicaragua was able to obtain an unheard of renegotiation of its foreign debt thanks to the political support received from the United Nations; and in 1983 Nicaragua was elected a member of the United Nations Security Council. Its legal suit brought about by the CIA's 1983 mining of its harbors has been accepted by the International Court of Justice at The Hague. In 1984, Nicaragua signed the Contadora Treaty, an action that received broad international support. Also in 1984, Nicaragua was named to the vice-presidency of the Inter-American Defense Council. In addition, it has been able to count on the material solidarity of countries also facing a serious economic crisis; Nicaragua has an international legitimacy that all of the Reagan administration's ideological apparatus and flagrant pressures have not been able to undermine. This legitimacy is directly related to the growing de-legitimization of the imperialist policies being put into practice against this small, heroic country.

The Sources of Legitimacy

The revolutionary leadership is legitimized to the extent that it is able to consolidate revolutionary power, keeping open the possibility for the people to transform society, build more just economic structures, develop social and individual freedoms, and guarantee national self-determination. Thus the deactivation of and final victory over the armed counterrevolutionary forces is a crucial component of this legitimization.

Another basic element is the form and content of governmental policies themselves and their popular stamp, the tendency to improve the living conditions of the majorities in both absolute and relative terms, and the clear possibility of the minorities to accommodate themselves within the revolutionary project.

But the crucial political element is the systematic search for and implementation of paths for making it possible for the increas-

4

ingly more organized people to become the revolutionary subject, thus losing their condition as a "mass" of atomized citizens without identity, who are summoned together but who lack autonomy.

In almost six years, the revolutionary government has made advances but has also had important limitations. Even though these advances are clear to those who wish to see them, and there are obvious explanations as to why further advances were not made in each case, material frustrations persist in the daily lives of Nicaraguans. Death continues to be present, because although Somocism has been overthrown as a regime, it persists as a counterrevolution openly fed by the Reagan administration. On the other hand, it is far from having achieved the satisfactory participation by and emancipation of the masses.

For this reason, one could be surprised that at the same time the revolutionary government fights against military attacks, the economic boycott, and the counterrevolution's ideological struggle—all led by the most powerful government in the world—it has decided to abide by the original proposal of holding elections, thus raising the possibility that different sectors or even the members of the opposition could capitalize on dissatisfaction. In holding the elections, the political will of building a different type of society that does not fit into any of the known models is reaffirmed in a novel attempt to combine social revolution and democracy, drawing the attention and the excitement of a broad spectrum of progressive forces in the world.

The Innovations of the Sandinista People's Revolution

Even though historical development will show the effectiveness and the possibility of a later generalization of some of the paths that have been adopted, it is already plainly evident that the Sandinista People's Revolution breaks with preconceived patterns in many ways. First of all, the very way of arriving at power itself—combining the armed struggle with a hegemonic behavior—was able to incite the active and passive consensus of the broadest possible social spectrum of Nicaraguan society. In the second place, a project of national unity has been sustained that does not

5

exclude any social sector and is concretized, for example, in state policies aimed at maintaining a mixed economy. In the third place, and as a component of the former, it has been proposed that social control over surplus production be achieved through the state monopoly over the financial system and over foreign marketing and not through the generalized expropriation of the means of production, that is, without private enterprise disappearing. In the fourth place, its political behavior is characterized by flexibility, within a model we could call *hegemonic* and not *dictatorial*. Thus the revolutionary leadership has not confused reality with revolutionary ideology, recognizing the heterogeneity of the ideological and political camp both in the international and national spheres. The consolidation and development of revolutionary power supposes the recognition of other ideas and forces, the building of a consensus, and the recourse to dialogue.

Such a political practice is not easy in the midst of a serious world and regional economic crisis, which is aggravated by the foreign siege, when, in addition, impatience exists to further advance the revolution's achievements that were fought for over so many years. Thus the revolutionary government sporadically resorted to forms of coercion such as enforcing the Economic and Social Emergency Law against the directors of the Consejo Superior de la Empresa Privada (COSEP—High Council of Foreign Enterprise) and the Central de Acción y Unidad Sindical (CAUS—Confederation for Union Action and Unity) in late 1981 when the counterrevolution began the "Red Christmas" campaign and the FSLN's attempts to keep dialogue open in the National Forum were frequently boycotted by the opposition parties. The print and electronic media were subjected to censorship when the counterrevolutionary attacks and the crisis worsened. Also there was a kind of freeze against the classic forms of union struggles, given the necessity to maintain production levels and the desire to preserve the national unity project. In the same way, on the level of discourse, anti-imperialist rhetoric (and also, at times, antibourgeois rhetoric) tended to be emphasized in the face of the rhetoric used by U.S. diplomats and their domestic spokesmen, who dedicated themselves to presenting the Sandinista People's Revolution as a satellite of the Soviet Union and Cuba.

However, the balance is clear: A coherent position has actively been maintained internationally, keeping open the possibility of negotiations and avoiding falling into the trap of the constant provocations by the Reagan administration, the CIA, and the counterrevolutionaries who use Honduran and Costa Rican territories as their sanctuaries, and appealing to all legal recourses allowed by the international community for defending the rights of a nation to self-determination and to delegitimize the Reagan administration's actions. On the domestic level, a pluralist system has been implemented and maintained from the start, in relation to the political parties and social forces, both as regards the formation of the executive branch of government and the cabinet, the Council of State, the judicial system, and regarding unions and business organizations, schools and churches, in an attempt to create various spaces for dialogue and legal political confrontation. In the same way, the economic policy, analyzed dispassionately, clearly shows the decision to promote private production to the point that there was no lack of those who saw this policy as a windfall for capital. In the same way, both in the economic and political spheres, the rules of the game were constantly being established that took the form of national laws, substantially reducing the possibility of the discretionary use of power that is always opened by a revolutionary situation.

Recently the Sandinista People's Revolution confirmed another innovative aspect: the search for a combination of representative forms (elections to the presidency, vice-presidency, and the National Assembly) with forms of direct popular participation in the construction of a substantive democracy that combines economic socialization with the socialization of political power. This implies rebuilding a system of political parties at the same time as the mass organizations and other direct forms of popular participation in the administration of society are developed.

Some Contradictions of the Revolutionary Process

If we take the revolutionary government's starting point to be a civil society underdeveloped by decades of tyranny and a backward

7

state that was reduced to the role of exploiter at the service of the Somoza family, within the context of a dependent agro-export economy heavily biased toward the peasant and artisan sectors, and with a proletariat and bourgeoisie limited in their development as classes, we must admit that the tasks that the Sandinista People's Revolution has taken on are extremely difficult.

To start with, these very innovations allow for the development of social contradictions that easily lead the leadership to feel politically attacked by both the Right and factions of the Left and accused of being "social democrats" and "communists" at the same time. But this is a subjective form of expression of the objective contradictions of Nicaragua's particular revolutionary project. Under structural conditions of underdevelopment and faced with a concurrent situation of crisis, a substantial improvement in the majority's living conditions is proposed at the same time as it sustains the convergence of interests within the capitalist sectors. Against the background of a political society marked by patterns of behavior engendered by the Somoza tyranny, the opening of real possibilities of political pluralism and competition for power is attempted while attempts are made to guarantee popular hegemony to advance social transformation. Against the historical backdrop of a weak civil society, attempts are made to develop the mass organizations in order to consolidate the possibilities of a true people's power at the same time as developing the state in order to guarantee social control over surplus production and national self-determination in the face of foreign aggression. A true social transformation is attempted with the collaboration of the sectors whose particular interests are affected, while, at the same time, an attempt is made to crystallize these transformations into law and the rules of the game.

Given its central role as the leader of this process, it is not strange that the FSLN should appear not only as the heroic revolutionary vanguard but also as "the government" and therefore the target of criticisms made from different perspectives. It could not be otherwise because the FSLN finds itself where all the contradictions unleashed by social and political revolutions are condensed. But these contradictions are objective, and their development through the social and political struggles implied by the revolution underway cannot be resolved by a decision made by the FSLN nor by a collective decision made through elections, under penalty of stopping the revolution itself or of readopting classic models.

The Meaning of Legitimization

Many political observers of the Nicaraguan process have symptomatically concentrated on watching the true possibilities of a pluralism defined for the opposition. They were more concerned that a possibility should arise for the bourgeoisie to express its positions or to aspire to alternate in power than about the possibility of true pluralism in the very heart of the popular camp. In this sense, other contradictions should be emphasized that cannot be resolved through the mere formality of elections, even though they may be a component of participatory democracy as defined by Sandinism.

It is a matter of resolving the relations of the FSLN with the government, the mass organizations, and of all these bodies with the domestic and foreign opposition as a means of consolidating the possibility for the Nicaraguan people to be sovereign and to forge a self-determined nation through the process of the government's legitimization at home and abroad, a process of which elections are only a part.

The stated legitimization should overcome the mountain of objective contradictions unleashed by a project that intends to break with preestablished models for which neither prepared formulas nor sufficient antecedents exist. Thus the concept of legitimacy itself must be built on the basis of the specific reality of a revolution that simultaneously advances economic socialization and the effective socialization of power in favor of the majorities, at the same time as it sustains a pluralist democratic system domestically and nonalignment internationally.

Within the context of a region convulsed by the direct struggle against the system of imperialist domination, the Sandinista Revolution has posed very complex tasks for Nicaragua, whose ideological importance for Central America and for all of Latin America is evidenced by the Reagan administration's rhetorical virulence and by its shamelessly open struggle to kill it at the same time as it tries to dissuade other peoples from starting down the road to liberation. In a certain way, the possibility and legitimacy of the Latin American peoples' struggle against their oppressors is being put to the test today in Nicaragua.

Chapter 2

Democracy and Revolution in Nicaragua

Introduction

This chapter is an attempt to show a central aspect of the Sandinista People's Revolution: unity and simultaneity between democracy and social change. In this manner, in the first part, we maintain that the political revolution was not reduced to the overthrow of Somoza but rather that it is an equally or even more drawn out process than the social revolution. Without referring to an analysis of the discourse produced by the Sandinista leadership, I will try to sustain this position conceptually by interpreting and highlighting certain aspects of the real process now taking place in Nicaragua. The revolutionary project is not seen as an a prioristically determined and rigidly maintained discourse but as a complex of actual practices evolving through the practice of transformation itself.

In the second part, I develop the conceptual scheme that allows me to state that, in fact, in Nicaragua the socialist program has always been inseparable from the construction of a substantive democracy. A key part of this argument is the very concept of *power* and its "location" in society. The vision of the formation of power structures both in the state and in civil society's institutions suggests—confronting the dichotomy between representative democracy and direct democracy—that the basic condition for the exercise of a substantive democracy is the constitution of the people themselves as the revolutionary subject. I maintain that, in this sense, through its practice, the Sandinista People's Revolution reasserts the possibility of a democratic path to the construction of socialism.

In the third part, I illustrate this through the actual experience of almost six years of revolutionary government and, in particular, on reflecting on the response given to foreign aggression and the economic crisis. In short, my thesis is that the revolutionary leadership's political behavior should be seen as the development of a popular hegemonic practice that differs from the models usually associated with the "dictatorship of the proletariat." The sense of this hegemonic practice becomes clearer if, applying the concept of power to be developed later, I note that power has not been "taken" in Nicaragua but rather is under construction, in a constant worldwide struggle against imperialism and against nonrevolutionary practice and ideology still being reproduced in Nicaragua both in the state and civil society. In this sense, the construction of a revolutionary state is accompanied by the construction of a civil society, and both are accompanied by the birth of new practices, institutions, and ideologies in society. The constitution of a "people" as the revolution's active subject implies the development of relatively autonomous mass organizations, given the need to guarantee the possibility of continuing the revolutionary process in the face of foreign aggression and the persistence of the tendencies to reproduce the old society. The characterization of the subject as a heterogenous popular collective leads me to pose the question of the role of the proletariat and to come to the conclusion that there is no contradiction between the proletariat's worldwide anticapitalist historic project and the popular national project underway in Nicaragua. In addition, I will point out some central questions pertaining to the process of building a substantive democracy in Nicaragua. Some of the problems derived from the political contradictions within the popular camp itself are discussed in general terms. It is shown that in Nicaragua the Sandinista People's Revolution has still not resolved but has drastically redefined the "national question" from the perspective of popular hegemony. In the same way as the peasant or ethnic questions are usually raised (as a question of their integration or dissolution), by analogy it is

12

posed that there is a "bourgeois question" in Nicaragua, that is, the possibility of reproducing private capital in a subordinated manner, at the same time as its owners are alienated as a political class. I then return to the central question of the creation of a hegemonic subject as the relation between the mass organizations and the revolutionary party. Reference is also made to the new phase of institutionalization, pointing out that the electoral process should be seen as a moment in the institutionalization process that began the very day of the revolutionary triumph. In addition, there is a discussion regarding some speculations about the dangers that combining representative mechanisms with those of direct democracy supposedly represent for the revolution.

The fourth part is a short methodological note about the limits of this work, pointing out the difficulties faced when analyzing a society during the first phases of transition.

Democracy and Social Revolution in the Periphery

The Democratic Program and Revolutions in the Periphery

In its weakest definition, the term *democracy* is usually reduced to the realm of politics and is associated with the notion of the *majority* insofar as it is identified with the election of governmental representatives by these majorities (representative democracy). Under this formal scheme, universal suffrage is considered to be the basic demand in systems that, for diverse reasons (race, gender, age, literacy, etc.), broad sectors of the population are denied the right to vote. The "right to vote" is presented as a human right—not to say a "natural" right—that is essential to this restricted and formalist view of democracy.

The truth is that, in the countries of the periphery, the majorities suffer material misery, political oppression, and ideological alienation, and the effective possibility of choosing their rulers is in fact limited. But even in systems with a long history of parlamentarianism (inherited in many cases from the colonial regime itself), periodic elections have not been effective for transforming the structures that oppress, exploit, and alienate these majorities.

13

Either through hegemonic procedures or through open dictatorship, the small minorities that control the means of production and circulation and the ideological and/or repressive apparata have been able to keep the majorities alienated from social power, even when they have occasionally had the opportunity to "veto" certain candidates or specific social projects.

Despite this, the scant development that formal democracy may have had in the world has not been so much the result of concessions or of bourgeois struggles as it has been of the struggles realized by the majorities themselves. Thus the growing extension of the right to suffrage of those who had previously been denied the franchise (women, ethnic minorities, youth, etc.) as well as its secret character should be recognized as popular demands. In reality, the oppressed and exploited have tried time and again to use the electoral system as a means for liberating themselves from military as well as subtle class dictatorships. But when, with the help of the colonial or imperial cities, the minorities block this path, the majorities are left with no other alternative but to resort to insurrection. That is to say, they express themselves as a social force capable of using violence for destabilizing and destroying a system of internal and foreign domination.[1] This right is seldom used anyway. But when a revolution does take place, the very system of parliamentary democracy (nationally or in the metropolis) that had been used to keep the majorities oppressed is questioned. It should not surprise us then that as part of the process of building a new society, new systems of regulation and social participation are sought that are superior to parliamentary forms.

But equally or more important than the establishment of these systems is the development that has taken place within the masses who have organized and constituted themselves as the revolution's real subject, thus overcoming their condition of being the "masses." In my judgment, this is the main criterion for establishing a program of substantive democracy in the periphery. Theoret-

---

1. It is worth noting that many liberal constitutions mention the right to insurrection. This is one of the social rights that cannot be pigeonholed in the category of "human" rights.

14

ically, this implies putting the masses and not the leaders in the center of analysis. On the contrary, to maintain that the small minorities will always be the makers of history, that the state is the "place" where the power for transforming or reproducing society is found—particularly when talking about these unstructured, "gelatinous" societies—and that the role of the masses is reduced to choosing those who should occupy this place through suffrage (passive support) or through insurrection leads us to a poor theory of democracy and to a poor and formalist democratic program.

But to surpass formalism in the conception of democracy immediately raises the need to recover unity between economics and politics, between society and the state, and between political revolution and social revolution. Thus, far from being reduced to the economic sphere, the socialist program does not reject all concepts of democracy as "bourgeois" but articulates the struggle for a substantive democracy with the struggle for social transformation because its theory demonstrates that they are inseparable.

The Socialist Revolution and Revolutions in the Periphery

THE "LOCATION" OF POWER

The concept held of power plays a central role in the explanation of what I could call the "socialist program." For some, the exercise of coercion and ideological domination are located in the state apparata. Thus the "taking of power" is understood to be the occupation of said apparata by a particular social group. For others, power structures are not only reproduced in and by the state apparata but also within civil society itself: in the schools, the church, the family, corporative organizations (business associations and unions), the media, the organizations dedicated to production and circulation, and so forth. Therefore, if we can talk at all about "taking power," it is in the sense of a long process that precedes and follows the displacement of rulers and their armed forces.

These alternative visions are also associated with socialist programs of different contents. Under the first concept, a particular program is visualized as the entire spectrum of social transforma-

15

tion—basically in the economic base—leading to the imposition of a new social logic. But in the same way that political power is conceived as being associated with the occupation of specific apparata, economic control is basically conceived of as the socialization of property (via its nationalization or cooperativization). At the same time, the impossibility of transforming the "superstructure" in the peripheral societies through the development of the economic base and its contradictions leads to raising the necessity of phases: first, the political revolution (the taking of power); then, the socioeconomic transformation led by the state. Only after the material base for a new society had been obtained would it become possible to dissolve the apparata of state power (the second political revolution).

The second concept denies the possibility of separating economics from politics. First of all, power is not located in a special apparatus, isolated from economic institutions, social reproduction, and the like. Second, the consolidation of revolutionary power requires advances in the building of a new people's power within civil society that cannot be condensed into the historical instant of the insurrection but rather implies a long process. Given the disperse character of power structures, they can only be "popular" when broad sectors of the population participate directly in their exercise, implementing a common national project. Thus the socialization of power and economic socialization go together, without having phases. The socialization of power implies overcoming the "massification" of the people—both that that the fiction of the "citizen" generates in liberal democracy as well as that that momentarily arises in the moment of the insurrection—in a process that is inseparable from the constitution of the "people" as the active revolutionary subject. This supposes articulating the different class identities in the popular camp but also other differences that, far from being obstacles for the constitution of this subject, are the basis for the mobilization and organization of the social forces that carry out the task of transforming society from the state and from civil society. "Articulation/unification," then, is not so much a matter of ideological decision and "project" as it is of the need for an active collective practice of struggle and construction of the material and ideological bases of the new society. Under this concept, the "passive" support of the governed is a hindrance from the past. It is a matter of mobilizing, activating, and incorporating all members of society who make up this revolutionary subject: the people, in the sense that I will develop later, into the process of transformation.

FORMS OF POWER AND THEIR LEGITIMIZATION

Representative Democracy. Starting from the historical premise that the people are the sole bearers of sovereignty, practical matters raise the question of its delegation to groups that (supposedly) exercise it in their name. Thus the theme of representation has a special place in the discussion of democracy. Going even further, the procedure for selecting representatives has come to be identified as that that summarizes the problem of democracy, taking as fact that "democracy is representative, or it does not exist." Elections—preferably on the basis of universal suffrage—have thus been converted into a synonym of "democracy." However, and even accepting the model of representative democracy, other aspects more or equally important than the electoral mechanism should be taken into account. The content of the policies implemented by the government and the projects advanced for social reproduction or transformation should be the object of a substantial evaluation. The legitimacy of a government cannot exclusively or fundamentally depend on how it came to govern but rather on the form in which the "public sphere" is handled, on how contradictions between particular interests and between these and the general interest are regulated, and naturally, how the "general interest" is determined. This last factor presents an obvious relativism, inasmuch as this evaluation will depend simultaneously on the position of the observer and his or her particular interests. In this search, the "objective" methods of evaluation, voting, and the electoral process have been posed as the procedures whereby, apparently, there would be no mediation between the collective will and decisions.

But history shows us an evident contradiction produced in parlimentary democracies where, by casting a vote or by abstaining, the majorities may ratify governments run by minorities that not only do not purport a popular social project but present a project that objectively suits their own particular interests. This validation has led to extending the concept of *hegemony* that was originally conceived to describe the relation between the proletariat and the other classes and popular sectors to the exercise and legitimization of power by the bourgeoisie.[2]

I start with the thesis that the struggle for popular power within a representative democracy hegemonized by the bourgeoisie should be oriented not only toward the "taking" of state power in a limited sense but also to disputing with the bourgeoisie for moral leadership in each one of the institutions of civil society where social consciousness (individual and collective, particular and universal) is forged. But this consciousness, that theoretically may be developed and diffused by a social class starting with the defense of its interests, is not necessarily—and much less mechanically—generated in recurring practices that are realized in the diverse social institutions. Thus the alternative that a political and ideological vanguard may assume this "possible consciousness" is opened as the political subject that temporarily precedes the historical subject[3] and struggles "in representation" of one class or social camp.

How is the legitimacy of this representation verified? On the one hand, it is verified by the development of the struggle itself, by its efficacy in transforming consciousness and deactivating the enemy's mechanisms of domination, and by the capacity of exercising leadership in critical situations, as seen, for example, in the moment of the insurrection. However, efficacy in the struggle cannot be the only criterion, in the same way that the efficacy of bourgeois domination does not validate this regime from a popular perspective. There are then more general criteria, such as those determined by a revolutionary social theory, which should be ap-

2. Humberto Cerroni, *Teoría política y socialismo* (Mexico: Editorial Era, 1976).

3. About this topic, see Orlando Núñez, "La revolución social y la transición en América Central: El caso de Nicaragua," a lecture given at the Fifth Central American Congress of Sociology, San Jose, Costa Rica, November 1982.

plied with the same rigor used to characterize the oligarchic or bourgeois regime, warning against the possibility of reproducing the old structures under new forms or facing the subreptitious reestablishment of an antipopular regime. However, in my judgment, the most relevant practical criterion is derived from an examination of the process of the constitution of the revolution's social subject, that is, of the "people" and their development as a political subject, which constitutes a formidable revolutionary task when starting with civil societies such as those that predominate in the periphery.

In any case, it is clear that the legitimacy obtained initially through the insurrection, far from being guaranteed by resorting to electoral mechanisms, requires other tests, particularly in the societies of the periphery.

Direct Democracy. The constitution of civil society and the "political emancipation" of individuals turned into citizens presupposes a contradiction in the practice of representative democracy: the contradiction between apparent political equality and the fact that the system creates and reproduces a division between a political elite that exercises the sovereignty it has been delegated and those it supposedly represents. The separation between the sphere of "politics" and the sphere of "private" institutions is a powerful ideological and institutional tool used by the dominant minorities to maintain majority consensus.

Breaking with this duality is a basic task of revolutionary criticism. On the one hand, this criticism implies pointing out situations in which the so-called "general interest" is in reality the private interests of the minorities combined with certain elementary concessions to maintain hegemony. On the other hand, it involves showing that the political structures of the state articulately extend and reproduce themselves as true relations of domination in what appears to be a realm of political equality in the institutions of civil society. The monopoly of scientific and technical knowledge accompanying the separation between manual and intellectual labor, ethnic, gender-based or generational subordination, the despotism of capital in labor relations, the despotism exercised by teachers in educational centers, the authoritarianism

19

of the hierarchy in religious communities, the unequal trade relations imposed by monopolies, and the like are but forms that coercion and repression take on in the very heart of so-called civil society, in addition to those that more obviously occur inside corporative organizations or political parties.

In more developed societies, these situations give way to resistance, demands, and the organization of social forces with common interests. These forces have a certain potential for taking action against the "system," but they also constitute the poles of a dialectical relationship within the system of domination itself. Thus we see that so-called "social movements" do not always constitute forces capable of revolutionizing society, even when they raise doubts about the efficacy of the system of political parties and of representative democracy for regulating social conflict. It is even possible that the system "reintegrate" them, as is the case with certain variants of the student, feminist, ecological, and pacifist movements. In the same way, decentralization (municipalization) has often been sponsored by reactionary central governments because this movement favors an even greater degree of separation between social participation and political control at the highest levels and provides a screen for the withdrawal of the "social" functions that the popular struggles wrested from the state in the past.

Even though this is not the place to go into more detail about these arguments, we can anticipate that even in a dense civil society, these partial struggles can hardly serve as a substitute for insurrection, given the system's ability to confront attacks "from within." On the other hand, obtaining the revolutionary triumph through a combination of counterhegemonic struggle and insurrection creates a situation that favors the establishment of a revolutionary democracy, but in no way does it provide solutions for all democracies' substantive problems.

For now, what is generally understood as "direct democracy"—that is, the assumption of functions and leadership positions at different levels by members of society directly affected by the power structure of which they are a part (factory councils, municipal governments, school boards, etc.)—is far from being revolutionary if it does not presuppose the formation of an authentic collective

20

subject that simultaneously holds these positions with a scientific view of globality, overcoming not only the alienation of the marketplace (or the centralized plan) but also the alienation of the particular movements, on the basis of a national project for liberation and for building a new society, explicitly discussed both in its tactical and strategic elements. In fact, the modern world hinders the building of a new society based on forms of local self-management when they are not combined with representative forms of local self-management and when they are not combined with representative forms at the national level that are capable of confronting national internal and external problems. An effective rotation in these representative positions and the constant effective control by the represented appear to be the only guarantees for assuring that such a society would not degenerate into hidden forms of the same system of political and social exclusion with which it is trying to break.

The liberal system simultaneously atomizes and socially massifies the majorities. A direct democracy conceived as local participation in the workplace, schools, and the like moves forward, but it still can fall into another level of massification if a qualitative leap is not made in building the collective subject. Heterogeneous in its class, ethnic, gender, cultural, religious, and other determinants but unified through national consciousness and the practice itself of social transformation, this subject creates its own material base and its own political regime. This requires organization on the basis of particular identities and the horizontal articulation of these popular identities, not only through social interchanges and the day-to-day nature of social interaction, but also explicitly through the exercise of sovereignty, of political and ideological discussion, and of the timely appropriation of science by the people themselves, developing their creativity in an organized manner. The Nicaraguan revolution can be visualized as an experience that is proving the possibility of simultaneously articulating political democracy and social transformation in favor of the masses. At the same time, it proves the possibility of simultaneously moving forward in the development of direct and representative forms of democracy. This is an important novelty in the area of the struggle for socialism because it reflects the old schemata of the necessary

21

"stages" according to which the development of certain material and social bases—the transformation of social structures, the implementation of a new logic for the production and distribution of goods, and the reaching of certain minimal levels in meeting the people's needs—would be a prior condition for moving forward with political and ideological democratization. The concept that the Nicaraguan experience in fact poses is that the alienation of the masses does not mechanically arise from their material living conditions and the conditions of production but rather that it is also produced by the absence of a democratic practice and that liberation requires simultaneous advances in both fronts of transformation.

The Nicaraguan revolution in fact poses the unity during transition of economics and politics of the class struggle—that does not freeze up because classes continue to exist but under new forms—and the struggle for dominating nature and developing the productive forces. It also conjugates political struggle against any form of dominating the workers with the formation of a new social (revolutionary) ideology that articulates revolutionary theory and practice, with no dogma other than the principle of defending the interests of the working classes. These majorities that stop being abstract convert themselves into the principal subject of the people's liberation.

The Sandinista People's Revolution

The Social Nature of the Sandinista People's Revolution

No one doubts that the Sandinista People's Revolution was an anti-Somocist political revolution. But it is not so clear to everyone—including some left-wing critics—that it was also a social revolution. It was a revolution against the dictatorship that was also against all forms of domination and exploitation of the working classes by the minorities. Nor is it so evident that the political revolution—inseparable from an authentic social revolution—is still an ongoing process.

The diagnostic made by the Sandinista National Liberation

Front showed that the prevailing social system—with or without Somoza—was incapable of majorities' most elementary needs or of returning national sovereignty to the Nicaraguan people.[4] At the same time, the history of Nicaraguan elections, "supervised" by U.S. Marines, demonstrated the impossibility of imposing the will of the masses through this means. As a result, during eighteen years the FSLN sustained a prolonged struggle against this regime personified by the Somoza family, demonstrating with its very existence the possibility of defying the system of repression created and sustained by the U.S. government. During the final phase of the war, in a series of events that is no doubt well-known,[5] diverse social forces and sectors joined in a broad anti-Somoza front, which was finally brought to victory by a general insurrection under the FSLN's leadership.

This final convergence confused many observers and some of the actors about the social character of the Sandinista People's Revolution. This confusion was made even greater when the FSLN, through its actions, confirmed the political decision to adopt popular hegemony as the constitutive characteristic of the transition to a new society, differentiating itself in this way from what has come to be known in the predominant practice of the socialist systems as the "dictatorship of the proletariat."[6]

At the same time as it was the result of a specific process, the revolutionary triumph was also a starting point for the development of a new correlation of social forces expressed in a political system hegemonized by the popular sectors. Subsequent actions irreversibly consolidated this correlation, thus resulting in the

4. See Jaime Wheelock and Luis Carrión, *Apuntes sobre el desarrollo económico y social de Nicaragua* (Managua).

5. See, for example, *Nicaragua, la estrategia de la victoria* (Mexico: Editorial Nuestro Tiempo, 1980).

6. The theoretical concept of the "dictatorship of the proletariat" is usually interpreted with a negative connotation due to the term *dictatorship*. However, as various authors have pointed out, it should be understood in the spirit that the term had when it was coined, which differs from the practice it is used to describe in most of the socialist countries. See Cerroni, *Teoría política y socialismo.*

23

political conditions for developing the process of building a new social system.[7]

The Sandinista People's Revolution's Political Practice

HEGEMONY AS A POLITICAL SYSTEM

It is clear that, during the struggle for power, certain abilities toward, and styles of, building a new society are molded. In its struggle against Somoza, the FSLN combined the armed struggle with counterhegemonic methods[8] in order to actively accumulate forces and to strengthen its legitimacy and, in defeating the regime, it simultaneously defeated the bourgeoisie's aspirations to win social hegemony "without Somoza." After the triumph, along these same lines of action, the possibility for all social sectors to actively participate in the new national project under revolutionary hegemony remained open.

It was a matter of carrying out a social revolution without physically annihilating the oppressors nor destroying the dominant class, but on the contrary, to call on them to cooperate and to transform themselves, integrating themselves into the process of national liberation. Some, confused by this attitude, believe (or pretended to believe) that the common opposition to Somoza in the final moments had erased history, putting all social sectors on the same political and moral footing and that now society would continue along its previous course—only without the "style" of domination that Somoza had given it.

7. Here I will concentrate on the political aspects of the Sandinista revolution. In other works I consider some of the economic aspects of the social transformation and the new system of accumulation resulting therein. See J. L. Coraggio, "Estado, política económica y transición en Centroamérica (notas para su investigacion)" [San Jose] 13, No. 37 (January-April 1984) and "Economics and Politics in the Transition: Reflections on the Nicaraguan Experience," eds. R. Fagen, C.D. Deere, and J. L. Coraggio (New York: Monthly Review Press, forthcoming in 1986).

8. Humberto Ortega Saavedra, *Sobre la insurrección* (Mexico: Ed. Nuestro Tiempo, 1980). Also see Amalia Chamorro, *Algunos rasgos hegemónicos del somocismo y la Revolución Sandinista, Cuadernos de Pensamiento Propio*, Essay Series, 5 (1983).

In its desire to sustain a program of national unity, the FSLN had to exercise a regulating function over social conflicts, in the name of the new state under construction. The first months of the revolutionary government were characterized by, among other things, holding back certain forms of class struggle, especially the attempts made to expropriate the direct control over the means of production from the bourgeoisie, regardless of its economic and political behavior.[9] Private ownership of the means of production was legally protected with the sole condition that it fulfill its social function in the new project—to produce. The revolutionary government continually proposed alternative routes for negotiation, participation, and dialogue; it systematically gave privilege to the mechanisms of consensus and persuasion, minimizing the use of repressive mechanisms.[10] At the same time, this confused others, for whom social revolution necessarily implied the generalized expropriation of the means of production, either by nationalizing them or turning them over to an immediate system of worker self-management. These left-wing sectors posed the possibility of a "Mexicanization" of the revolution as a real danger threatening the revolutionary process.

Even in view of this, certain members of the bourgeoisie refused to accept the popular revolutionary hegemony from the start, trying to put themselves at least on the same footing as all the sectors that took part in the final stage of the insurrection. Their

9. On November 21, 1979, the FSLN delivered a communique condemning the "gangs" that were acting in the name of the revolution, ordering an immediate suspension of confiscations and seizures of residences, vehicles, and urban and rural property until the legal ordering and administration of what has been confiscated and seized until now has been concluded. (See *Barricada*, 21 November 1979.) Orlando Ruiz, director of the Nicaraguan Chamber of Commerce, responded to the suspension of Decree No. 38 that referred to the status of goods and property held by people "allied with Somocism" with the following comment: "With this measure, a climate of confidence is guaranteed at the commercial and industrial level. A climate of political tranquility, even though the climate of economic tranquility is not well established" (*Barricada*, 23 November 1979).

10. See Salvatore Senese, "Aspetti giuridicci del nuovo assetto politico sociale," in *Relaziones presentate alle giornate di studio sul Nicaragua* (Rome: Fundazione Lelio Basso, April 1981).

25

concept of the "revolution" was void of social content, in that it was reduced to the overthrow of Somoza. Soon the accelerated formation of the mass organizations and of the Sandinista People's Army gave an unmistakable social content to the revolution, which was noticed from the start by these sectors. That is why, up until the end, they had tried to save the National Guard with the goal of neutralizing the revolutionary forces once Somoza had fallen. In turn, the Carter administration did not hesitate in signaling this sector that it was "on their side." This prompted them to immediately begin an ideological struggle based on the same anticommunist slogans used by Somoza.[11] However, given the FSLN's ability to establish its political hegemony, these sectors—the same ones who today call the ex-national guardsmen "rebels," those who were urged on from Honduras by imperialism—were unable to create an internal political front around a project that would neutralize the revolutionary project's class content. Thus the productive response of the private owners was generally positive[12] in the face of the combination of persuasion, economic incentives, and the definition of legal limits on the rights to private property and within the context of a correlation of forces that deprived the bourgeoisie of an internal armed wing.

PLURALISM WITHIN THE REVOLUTION

A hegemonic system implies the existence of pluralism, but in every social system pluralism is limited. The question then is who

11. By December 1979, rumors had already begun to fly in Nicaragua that there were shortages of meat and basic grains because these products were being sent to Cuba! On December 12 of that year, the U.S. House of Representatives approved a highly debated $75-million credit but threatened to suspend it "if Cuban or Soviet troops are stationed in Nicaragua."

12. Since the revolution, production of coffee, sugar, rice, sorghum, and other crops has reached unprecedented levels. In the case of sugar, the state holds fifty percent of production, but in other products the private sector heavily predominates. The low level of private investment that the revolution's detractors point to as an indication of the lack of a positive political "climate" is similar or even higher than in other Central American countries affected by the crisis of the Central American common market, particularly in their industrial sectors.

sets these limits and in what form, a problem that is clearly determined by the correlation of forces as well as by the nature of the principles that guide those in power.

In the case of Nicaragua, pluralism's existence cannot be denied. But this pluralism explicitly excludes Somocism and those groups willing to turn over national sovereignty to foreign forces. No social group or class as such is excluded from the political system.

From the very beginning, pluralism existed in the government (in the makeup of the government junta and the cabinet, and among government officials in general), in the Council of State,[13] the judicial system, the mass media (radio and print), in the unions and business associations, the churches, the educational apparatus, the system of political parties, in the National Council of Political Parties, and so on. This pluralism includes both the different social and political positions existing within the popular camp as well as the "opposition." This opposition is within the hegemonic system itself in that, in general, it shares anti-imperialism and anti-Somocism, even though it may have broad differences regarding political, economic, and ideological questions.[14] The minorities can express their particular demands, fight for greater representation in the institutions, and present their alternatives for the country. But when their actions are aimed at subordinating the people's interests to their own particular interests under the leadership of a bourgeoisie in the opposition that is associated with imperialism, then they find resistance not only from the FSLN but from the popular organizations also.

On the other hand, although the FSLN may maintain total control over the army, the Sandinista People's Militia has been an open door of access to the armed forces, a fact that has no parallel

13. In May 1981, eight political parties, seven union organizations, three mass organizations, six producers' organizations, and several other organizations were represented in the Council of State. About the discussion regarding the change in the council that took place in 1980, see Senese, *Aspetti giuridici.*

14. For more information about pluralism in Nicaraguan institutions, see *Pensamiento Propio* 1, nos. 6 and 7 (July-August 1983).

27

in the rest of the so-called "democratic" countries of Latin America.

If there are structural limits to pluralism found in every society, in a process of structural transformation there will always be sectors that will see some of their old "rights" being violated and who will resist being subordinated or reintegrated into civil and political society. For this reason, the need to appeal to the difference between pluralism "within the revolution"—that is, within a new hegemonic system—and a supposedly universal and ahistorical pluralism, is obvious. This latter version is in reality an ideological stepping stone for those who wish to reduce the insurrectional majorities to the condition of being a tool for the interests of their own faction.

HEGEMONIC BEHAVIOR IN CRITICAL SITUATIONS

In any case, the method of hegemony, the maintenance of pluralism, cannot be captured merely by examining the structures of participation or the legal system. Only the dynamic of the social process in the postrevolutionary triumph period will allow us to see if this is a substantive and permanent characteristic of the revolutionary project or if it is only a means for "gaining time."

Certainly, in the case of Nicaragua, the facts demonstrate the first alternative. Let us take as an example the analysis of two situations recently juxtaposed in the Nicaraguan political scene: (a) the threat of a direct invasion by the U.S. Marines and (b) the economic crisis Nicaragua faces together with the rest of the Central American countries.

The Threat of a U.S. Invasion. In the face of the escalating armed actions being carried out by the counterrevolutionary forces coming from Honduras and Costa Rica and the certainty that a U.S. invasion of Nicaragua was being prepared just after the invasion of Grenada, a series of measures were taken that contradicted what were widely anticipated as the expected responses to such a critical situation.

Keeping in mind the experiences of the Popular Unity government in Chile and the Manley government in Jamaica, the print and electronic media were subjected to prior censorship. However, the main opposition newspaper was not closed as many had de-

28

manded, and censorship was eased as soon as the overall situation permitted.[15]

Not only was the executive branch not centralized, but it was further decentralized, allowing for greater democratization within the state and for a greater degree of participation and control over the government by civil society on the regional and local levels.

Agrarian reform was speeded up in favor of the peasant population, even when this went against the basic criterion of efficiency (inability of the state to provide sufficient supplies, services, etc.) and despite the fact that the land affected was largely state owned. Thus conditions were created that in the future would strengthen socialization via cooperativization and would slow down the process of proletarianizing the peasantry.

The process of popular organization and of access to weapons ("All Arms to the People") were notably intensified both in quality and quantity, and in addition, territorial militias were formed. All this is implicit proof of a level of confidence in the people that few governments could withstand.

What is closely related to the last three points is that some of the mass organizations were strengthened. This will have an enormous influence on the development of the revolution, as is the case of the Comités de Defense Sandinista (CDS—Sandinista Defense Committees) and the Unión Nacional de Agricultores y Ganaderos (UNAG—National Farmers and Cattlemen's Union). Since its inception, UNAG has demonstrated a great degree of autonomy and strength as well as a critical spirit within the revolutionary process.

Despite the war situation, state economic intervention has been maintained at the minimal necessary level. When it became possible, some products were taken off the ration list; differential pricing mechanisms were introduced to regulate the distribution

15. In addition, we should look at the exact extent of the censorship that was implemented. The newspaper *La Prensa*, voice of the opposition (when not directly the voice of the U.S. administration), could exhibit the censored pages on its bulletin boards and send copies to embassies and other institutions in Managua. Mostly, war-related news and stories that might create panic due to the lack of supply of goods and thus feed the black market are censored.

of gasoline; there were no incursions against private property based on generic reasons of "national security"; and the system of economic incentives given to productive capital was not only maintained but emphasized.

Demagogic measures were not taken, such as a generalized wage increase that could not be supported by the supply of consumer goods, in spite of a request made for such an increase by the Sandinista unions.

The financial control of the state businesses was broadened, continuing a tendency of giving equal treatment to state and private businesses and reducing bureaucracy. The discussion of the political parties statute and the electoral calendar continued along the lines announced in 1980, and the process was neither speeded up nor slowed down. Later, once the danger of an imminent invasion had passed, it was announced that the elections would be moved up to November 1984.

All internal and external channels of negotiation were kept open, and a veritable peace offensive was undertaken to demonstrate the will to end the armed conflict.[16] At the same time, armed actions were strictly limited to defending national territorial integrity, to avoid an irreversible regionalization of the war, even when an invasion that would have this as its final result seemed imminent.

In summary, both what was done and what was not done show the tactical position the FSLN holds, in the sense that foreign aggression must be confronted, above all by maintaining a broad anti-imperialist national front, hegemonized by the popular forces organized for the defense of national self-determination.

This confirmed the political position that the nation/empire opposition is central to the process of liberation, which on the domestic level means affirming popular sovereignty over the possibility of surviving as a government subject to imperialist hegemony.

16. See *Bases jurídicas para garantizar la paz y la seguridad internacionales de los Estados de América Central (propuesta oficial de Nicaragua a Contadora)* (Managua: October 15, 1983).

The Economic Crisis. The economic crisis affecting all of Central America[17] caused by the erosion of the terms of trade, the growing costs of the foreign debt, and the crisis of the Central American Common Market, is aggravated in Nicaragua by the legacy of Somocism and the war of liberation, the economic blockade imposed by the U.S. administration and its allies,[18] and the necessity of diverting more and more resources to the defense of the country against foreign aggression.

Faced with this situation, the policies designed by the revolutionary government to confront the crisis showed the following characteristics[19]: For the 1983–1988 period, a program of macroeconomic adjustments limiting public and luxury spending was proposed.

In contrast to the stabilization plans proposed by the International Monetary Fund (IMF), the harshest effects of the crisis were not to fall on the backs of the working class but rather on those sectors that had the highest income levels. It was decided that commitments to foreign creditors would be honored and actions would be taken to refinance the debt while maintaining the policy of making service payments as had been done until then.

The possibility of basing the functioning of the economy on disproportionate foreign subsidies did not appear in the proposal so that, in principle, the adjustment led to programming a negative growth rate of the per capita gross national product (GNP).

In contrast with neighboring countries where capital emigrated and investments were abandoned, an investment rate was proposed for Nicaragua that would keep open the possibility of economic recovery when the country emerged from the recession,

17. See *Regional Report for Central America*, an official document of the governments of Costa Rica, El Salvador, Guatemala, Honduras, and Nicaragua prepared in 1983 by the Inter-American Development Bank for the international financial community.

18. See Jim Morrel and Jesse Biddle, "Central America: The Financial War," a study presented at the Seminar on Political Alternatives for Central America and the Caribbean, Washington, D.C., December 1983. Also see their earlier report, published in *International Policy Report*, March 1983.

19. See *Lineamientos de política económica 1983–1988* (Managua: Junta de Gobierno de Reconstrucción Nacional, 1983).

without an irreversible deterioration of the productive apparatus. The predicted profit rates followed the pattern of the prior two years, guaranteeing an important profit margin to private capital, even under conditions of recession.

The process of a new socialization of the productive forces emphasized both the path of cooperativization of small- and medium-sized producers and the development of state-owned enterprises.

In regard to foreign trade, the tendency toward diversifying markets was to be maintained, keeping a balance between countries of the Third World, Western Europe and Japan, the United States, and the socialist countries.

In summary, even under conditions of a serious economic crisis arising from foreign and domestic factors (the war of liberation), we are witnessing a revolution with a program of socialist transformation that does not curtail efforts for remaining responsibly integrated in the world market, maintaining its legitimacy on the international political scene and, therefore, questioning the legitimacy of U.S. aggression. At the same time, it avoids falling into short-term demagogy, trying to assure permanent material bases for popular hegemony, and above all, resting on the national effort.

Even though this program had contradictory aspects, and, in the end, its implementation would face unavoidable difficulties due to the critical situation affecting the world and regional economy as well as due to the costs of the military aggression, we are interested in highlighting the political intentionality, which demonstrates a line of thought (both nationally and internationally) oriented by the concept of hegemony as a political system.

The Sociopolitical Meaning of the Revolution in Nicaragua

THE INITIAL CONDITIONS AND THE TASKS OF THE REVOLUTION

In July 1979, under the leadership of the FSLN, the people of Nicaragua won the possibility of carrying out a social and political revolution. Although they gained control over the fundamental components of the institutional structure absolutely necessary for carrying out this revolution, "power as such" in its multiple dimensions has yet to be integrally assumed or "taken," either by the FSLN or by the people.

Internationally, until July 1979, Nicaragua was almost directly dominated by U.S. imperialism, not so much as a place to invest capital but rather as the kingpin for the geopolitical domination of the Central American region. The participation of Somocism in the repression of popular movements in Costa Rica and Guatemala and in the Bay of Pigs was nothing more than a demonstration of this role. And, even though it was dealt a serious blow with the defeat of the National Guard, imperialism has not been overthrown. Its capacity for military, political, ideological, and economic coercion is enormous, and everything indicates that the current administration has made a genuine crusade out of repressing popular movements in Central America. But, on the other hand, the United States aspires to maintain its hegemony over the world capitalist system in crisis, and this puts certain limits on its foreign policies at the same time as it presents other possibilities for struggle for the Sandinista People's Revolution.

Domestically, even though it presented some "hegemonistic traits," the Somoza regime was far from being a hegemonic system because coercion and exclusion predominated over consensus and integration. Somoza's open dictatorship virtually "squashed" Nicaraguan society, hindering the development of a dense civil society and, at the same time, simplifying the state to the point where it had not even developed the mechanisms of economic control common to other Latin American countries. As a consequence, both for a concept that sees in the state an apparatus where power is located and for that that sees in civil society's institutions a complex network of relations that reproduce the structure of social power, it is evident that the building of revolutionary power in Nicaragua must be accompanied by the construction of the state and of civil society, which implies the development of new practices, behaviors, and ideologies at all levels.

There is another initial condition of great importance: The economic base with which Nicaragua inserts itself in the world market can not be drastically transformed, possibly for the remainder of this century. As a result, there is no objective possibility of massive urbanization or industrialization projects. Even though the natural and human conditions would allow for them, the pressure exerted by the present situation forces the reproduction of an agro-export model, at least in regard to the lines of production and their articulation in the world market. As a consequence, brusque changes should not be expected in the objective composition of the social classes. The quantitative predominance of the peasantry, small- and medium-scale cottage industry, and a broad layer of "informal" agents of circulation and services can be expected to persist for a prolonged period of time. Therefore, sociopolitical transformation should proceed along these lines.[20]

The building of popular power is then a formidable task for the future that not only assumes the need for armed resistance against the attacks by the Somocist guardsmen and the delegitimization of imperialist aggression worldwide, but it also requires the construction of a revolutionary state, the formation of a civil society (as a system of institutions and practices), and the development of the collective subject that will assume the moral leadership of these institutions for the popular camp, led by a hegemonic popular and national project.

THE SOCIAL PROJECT AND ITS SUBJECT

With the initial conditions already laid out and in the face of a marked escalation of imperialist aggression, conditions would appear to exist for the revolutionary leadership to adopt the path of temporarily centralizing power in the vanguard, the massification of the people, the dissolving of "anarchic" forms of private property, and the state's almost total control over the economic and political systems. However, the Sandinista project—as demonstrated by facts and discourse—has adopted the strategy of building and sustaining an economy that articulates various forms of production and a hegemonic system based on consensus and pluralism where the institutions of the state and civil society must be

20. For a further discussion of the social composition of the social subject of the insurrection, see the revealing work of Carlos M. Vilas, "El sujeto social de la insurrección popular y el carácter de la Revolución Sandinista," a lecture given at the XV Congreso Latinoamericano de Sociología Simón Bolívar, Managua, October 10–14, 1983.

developed and the subject and the interlocutor of this hegemony must be forged simultaneously. In this sense, the Sandinista People's Revolution has demonstrated that there is no universal relationship between imperialist aggression and the revolutionary project's content, affirming national self-determination.

The hegemonic method of building popular power has implied that the revolution responds to each new escalation by imperialism and the regional oligarchies by reaffirming the broad social and political spectrum that makes up the internal anti-imperialist front, strengthens popular hegemony, and also reaffirms its counterhegemonic behavior in the world political scene, delegitimizing the present U.S. administration in front of its own Western allies. This responds not only to a clear perception of the situation and of the most efficient means available but also to the maintenance of the principles of the Sandinista People's Revolution themselves, whose popular and national autochthonous nucleus (the legacy of Augusto C. Sandino) is of great importance for understanding these options.[21]

The observers who evaluate the revolution and its project should keep its difficulties in mind. We are talking about making a profound democratic revolution in a country that has just suffered one of the most bloody dictatorships that had been kept in power by successive U.S. administrations since Sandino's assassination. This prolonged dictatorship produced a weak government apparatus, incapable of even designing and implementing a weak Keynesian policy, given that Somoza's methods were direct and not very sophisticated. But it also produced a weak civil society, where the normal usage of the term *masses* gives an erroneous idea: It was far from having completed the liberal-democratic process of massification/homogenization of the population not only as "citizens" but also as producers and consumers. The absence of a meaningful democratic practice and the profound social, ideological, and cultural differentiations present in this society hindered its "spontaneous" organization. This also affected the bourgeoisie and the petit bourgeoisie, who looked to the "States" for educating

21. Augusto C. Sandino, *El pensamiento vivo de Sandino*, introduction and edition by Sergio Ramirez (Managua: Editorial Nueva Nicaragua, 1984).

their children, spending their money, and for ideological leadership.

If the National Reconstruction government had called for elections immediately after Somoza's overthrow, there possibly would
have been an even greater level of legitimacy among, for example,
its social-democratic friends. But, what would have been the significance and content of this act, beyond formally complying with
the "rules" of democratic behavior? Even now that the government
has carried out the program announced in 1980 of holding elections (which were even moved up), they cannot be the definitive
criterion of the democratic nature of its revolutionary project.

As a social revolution, starting from the very difficult conditions it inherited, the Sandinista People's Revolution has to be a
revolution of civil society: thus, it will be a profound political
revolution. Even though the FSLN's role as the provider of revolutionary leadership is undeniable, the subject of the revolution is
not given beforehand, but, rather, its development is itself one of
the revolution's goals. The organization of the masses means their
transformation and their constitution as the people. The multiple
identities of the Nicaraguan masses will be alienated, dominated,
and subordinated as long as they cannot express themselves as a
social force, pose their own demands and ideologies, and transform themselves through the social struggle that is the revolution
in process.[22] For the Sandinista People's Revolution, the building
of an hegemonic system means therefore developing and liberating
the people's various identities.

But recognizing the differences that exist within the masses is
not enough. Revolutionary hegemony depends on autonomous
organization and, at the same time, on articulating specific social
forces around a popular project for the nation (and its insertion in
the world system), which makes them universal. This project,
recovering the peculiarities of a popular and national being, can-

22. On this subject, see Chapter 3 of this book. The hegemonic process
has an unequal development due to its contradictory character, but for the
same reason, the liberation of the people's identity implies their simultaneous transformation. And when we talk about the transformation, we have in
mind that there are at least two parties involved in the relation that defines
an identity and that both parties undergo deep ideological and behavioral
changes.

not be given beforehand, except in the strategic lines that the revolution's very nature marks with clarity. Instead, it will become concrete along with the development of the people's creative capacity.

It is not a coincidence that, from the start, the opposition sectors of the bourgeoisie, such as the COSEP, aimed their ideological artillery at what they called the "illegality" of the mass organizations. Obviously, the constitutive moment of a people cannot be based on the legalities of an oppressive system with which a definitive rupture is desired. The Unión Nacional de Agricultores y Ganaderos (UNAG—National Farmers and Cattlemen's Union), the Central Sandinista de Trabajadores (CST—Sandinista Worker's Confederation), the Asociación de Trabajadores del Campo (ATC—Farmworkers' Association), the Asociación de Mujeres Nicaragüenses "Luisa Amanda Espinoza" (AMNLAE—Luisa Amanda Espinoza Nicaraguan Women's Association), the Juventud Sandinista 19 de Julio (JS19J—July 19 Sandinista Youth Organization) and, above all, the Comités de Defensa Sandinista (CDS—Sandinista Defense Committees) infuriated those who intended to rebuild the old coalition of forces. And they had good reasons for their anger. If we further add the development of the Milicias Populares Sandinistas (MPS—Sandinista People's Militia)—these "armed citizens" who are difficult to classify in the state/civil society dichotomy—and the attempt to unify the ethnic minorities in a common organization called MISURASATA (Miskitos, Sumos, Ramas, and Sandinistas United), it is obvious that, from the start, far from seeking its own self-perpetuation as the only political power, the FSLN had undertaken the development of the revolution's subject—the people. At the same time, this development is the consolidation of an irreversible popular hegemony. The revolutionary task proposed by the FSLN was not, then, that of merely building a modern state but rather that of articulating these identities and preventing their manipulation in the interests of imperialism and the reactionary minorities.[23]

At the same time, the Sandinista People's Revolution attempted to seek a provisional institutional form for a process that

23. In this sense, in the eventuality of a U.S. invasion, the possibility of a repetition of the Grenadian tragedy in Nicaragua does not exist, given the

has still to be resolved in Europe: the articulation between political parties and social movements. Thus the Council of State that had co-legislative functions included representatives of the political parties, corporate and union organizations, and nontraditional social movements.[24]

THE ROLE OF THE PROLETARIAT[25]

It may be possible to question the apparent nonclass character of the Sandinista People's Revolution that has been outlined so far. However, as soon as the discussion is placed within the currents that purport the need to overcome dependent capitalism and to create another type of society—another form of economic and polit-

---

power and the autonomy the mass organizations have already obtained and their articulation with the revolutionary project. On the other hand, the example of the Miskitos points out a case in which the FSLN could not avoid the manipulation of this identity by imperialism. Now, even though the FSLN has recognized its "errors" in the treatment of this problem, the truth is that the question of integrating the ethnic minorities at the same time as preserving their autonomy has never been satisfactorily resolved in Latin America. The Latin American Left itself has vacillated between the extremist position of identifying these minorities with the proletariat (thus seeing their complete proletarianization as the "solution to the problem") and another extremist position that adopts an "indigenousphile" stance according to which the total self-determination and even the territorial autocracy of these communities should be accepted as a counterpart of "white" society. When a revolution such as Nicaragua's takes place, the possibility of seeking a new focus for the ethnic question opens up. Unfortunately, the fact that the counterrevolution infiltrated precisely into the zones where the Miskitos lived at the same time as certain religious leaders preached that "the revolution was the devil" produced situations whose treatment by the FSLN could not be seen simply as a "mistake" but rather as the necessary result of a real contradiction between defending the possibilities of the people as a whole to carry out their revolution, of defending it against foreign aggression, and the will to allow the Miskito's developing and slow articulation with the process of national liberation.

24. For more information, see *Pensamiento Propio* 1, nos. 6–7 (July– August 1983).

25. On this topic, see Orlando Núñez, "La revolución social y la transición" and also Ernesto Laclau, "Socialisme et transformation de logiques hégémoniques" and Chantal Mouffe, "Socialisme, democratie et nouveaux mouvements sociaux," in *La gauche, la pouvoir, le socialisme*, ed. Cristine Buci-Glucksman (Paris: PUF, 1983).

ical socialization that responds to the project of the oppressed and exploited sectors—the question of the role of the proletariat immediately arises. In societies in which the process of proletarization has been extremely incomplete and in which a good part of salaried work is far from being close to the model of an urban industrial proletariat, the possibility arises that the revolution's social and historical subjects do not coincide. It would then be a matter of other social forces assuming the historical project of the proletariat as the class that is structurally antagonistic to capital. Beyond any theoretical or ideological discussion, this is in fact what socialist revolutions in the capitalist periphery try to do.

The problem is if it should be the goal of the construction of a new society and its material bases to materially complete the process that capitalism did not finish in these societies: the development of the proletariat up to the point where it is effectively the dominant social force. This has two possible interpretations: Either the proletarian project is assumed in its broadest sense, that is, liquidating the exploitation or domination exercised by capital or rather literally assume that the only subject that can produce this transformation is the national proletariat, and, then, its constitution as the predominant class appears to be a prior condition for completing the revolution. This obviously implies a process of social homogenization, of proletarianizing the peasantry, of concentrating and proletarianizing the artisans, of culturally integrating the ethnic minorities, of ending differences in the work performed by men and women, of forming a national market and idiosyncrasies that surpass localisms and so forth—all of which would lead to the development of a revolutionary proletarian consciousness. But this process cannot be carried out without the effective development of capital because the condition of the proletariat is not an idealistic "attribute" but rather a material relation that supposes the existence of its opposite pole (private or state, national capital, or foreign capital).

When we raise this possibility in the context of small economies with a natural and demographic base that itself hinders the complexity of the capitalist development of the productive forces and their corresponding social agents and relations, such a proposal could well point more to a "marginalizing" development than to a "proletarianizing" development of the social structure. This proposal's economicist and generalist bias is clear in that such a *national* political and social strategy is based on an analysis of the tendential laws of capitalist development and its principal contradictions as a *world system*. But upon uniting economics and politics, the national revolutionary project in fact establishes the people (in the sense used here) *tendentially* as the revolution's social and political subject. The people (articulated by and with the vanguard) can assume the historical tasks of self-transformation in the anticapitalist struggle but starting with its heterogeneity and its particularities without forcibly denying them or homogenizing them, developing the national identity of the struggle in relation to the broader struggle taking place worldwide.

Numerous contradictions obviously exist within this collective subject, but the existence of a common historical project aids in overcoming them, without this requiring in any way a reduction—ideological or real—of the people to a class predetermined by its position in the structure of capitalist society. This is compatible with the statement that from the perspective of the overall movement of human society, such a project must be visualized as "proletarian" in that, on a national level, it encarnates—as a specific and always concrete project—the universal tendencies that will overcome the capitalist society that today predominates in the world.

Concretely, the peasant logic can also be anticapitalist, as can the struggles of women or of youth or of the ethnic identities. To prevent these individual demands or logics from being subordinated to capital and assuring that, instead, they constitute the forces of liberation, liberating themselves in the affirmation of a new society, is a revolutionary task.

The Problems of Constructing a Substantive Democracy in Nicaragua[26]

THE CONTRADICTIONS IN THE POPULAR CAMP

The problematic of democracy in Nicaragua cannot simply be presented in terms of a comparison between the actual institu-

26. See also Xabier Gorostiaga, *Los dilemas de la Revolución Popular Sandinista* (Managua: Cuadernos de Pensamiento Propio, 1982).

tional system or the projects for its transformation and a supposedly universal model (for example, the European parliamentary
system). It is rather a matter of analyzing and evaluating a system
of contradictions that occur in a process of social and political
transformation with the goals discussed previously, trying to establish the possible and desired development of such contradictions. Here we will limit ourselves to pointing out some of the
questions that the revolutionary process itself generates.

From a popular perspective,[27] the revolution must face the
following problems:

*(a) How to resolve the relationship between the government, the
political parties (especially the FSLN), and the mass organizations.*

In regard to the government/party relationship, it is a matter of
finding mechanisms through which government officials are basically accountable to the people and that the logic of government
organization does not become confused with the logic of party
organization.

In regard to the relationship between the party and the mass
organizations, the central problematic boils down to the question
of how to resolve the need to articulate the popular camp in order to
guarantee the defense of the revolution and the continuation of the
revolutionary process and, on the other hand, the need to guarantee the autonomy of the mass organizations to make a substantive
democracy possible. It is particularly difficult to resolve this contradiction in the context of foreign aggression and starting from a
historical situation of a barely developed civil society that confirms
the need for the revolutionary party's initiative and the impossibility of trusting sheer spontaneity.

(b) The form that the revolutionary party will finally adopt.

---

27. A large number of foreign commentaries about this topic have fo-
cused on the question of how to resolve the contradictions between the revolution and the "opposition," without paying much attention to the contradictions that arise within the popular camp itself.

Here two possibilities are opened up: that of the revolutionary party formed by cadres capable of assuming both the global political leadership of society as well as the specific tasks within the state and civil society with a common perspective or the alternative of the mass party that includes in its ranks all of those elements that share the basic aspects of the project that the party embodies but who in their whole form a broad spectrum of positions regarding specific situations of the revolutionary process.

Another fundamental aspect is the system of decision making in the heart of the party: Here verticalism and "basism" are counterposed as extremes. The history of revolutions has shown that the resolution of these alternatives is not a "private" question of the party, but rather it has pervasive effects on the social forms of political life.

Finally, another question intimately linked to the earlier ones is related to the class character of the revolutionary party: It will either assume a specific class or alliance as its own subrogated subject or will have the people, in the sense developed previously, as its subject. The first option does not imply leaving aside the path of popular hegemony, but rather it is a way of organizing itself to give this hegemony a more specific historical orientation, that is, a strategic classist orientation.

(c) The form of legitimization of individuals who take on leadership or representative positions in the parties and mass organizations.

This refers to the effective possibility of the people to choose, control, and eventually remove their representatives, avoiding bureaucratization and separating a self-perpetuating elite from the true repositories of sovereignty.

(d) The development of the capacity of the majorities to understand and control the social structures as well as to collectively design a hegemonic project, effectively appropriating scientific knowledge.

This is not merely a matter of "educating" the people, but rather

42

of developing methods of participation in which new abilities for management and understanding are forged. It is a revolutionary task that the entire people appropriate theory for establishing mediations between each particular situation and the national and world social globality. This is a necessary condition for being able to effectively participate in the design of a scientifically based project.

This implies the creation of forums for discussion, where the large challenges presented by social transformation can also be incorporated: the destiny of the peasantry, the means of resolving the contradictions between the city and the country, the options for international rearticulation, the options for technological development, the forms for popular participation, and the concretization of new relations of production, the question itself of the relationship between the revolutionary party, the state, and the mass organizations and the mechanisms of pluralism and so forth.

(e) Effective democratization of the administration of the means of production and consumption.

This has to do with the articulation of the diverse forms and bodies of participation: worker self-management, worker participation in the administration of business, direct participation by the mass organizations in the decision-making bodies at a local, regional, and national level in the definition of social and economic strategies and their follow-up. How to accomplish them is another question that the revolution must resolve.

(f) The organized regulation and expression of contradictory individual interests and the collective definition of the "general interest" under a regime of popular hegemony.

This implies searching for forms of interconnecting regimes for political organization (parties, the parliament) with networks of social organizations around specific identities or concrete interests (mass organizations, but also the minority sectors' established organizations).

(g) The effective popular appropriation of the media.

This implies not only that the media will be directed at the masses, but it also guarantees the peoples' access to the media and opens the material possibility of creating their own specific means of communication and their forms of discussion about national or local, global or sectorial problems.

(h) A revolutionary institutionalization

This implies the continual institutionalization of the revolution, while maintaining the flexibility needed so that a crystallization of structures that could restrain the revolutionary process in the long run does not develop.

These and many other problems confronting a revolution take place in the very heart of the popular camp, and their resolution is a condition for guaranteeing the effectiveness of the popular hegemony that hinders—with a minimum of repressive mechanisms—the possibility for bourgeois minorities to either openly or surreptitiously regain control of the nation's economic, political, and cultural life. None of these questions—and to an even lesser degree, their whole—can automatically be resolved just by political will. This is a matter of a long process whose rhythm will be determined by a dialectic between the organized masses, the revolutionary party, the opposition within the revolution, and the enemy.

THE NATIONAL QUESTION

Normally the national question is associated with the formation of a self-determined, internally integrated nation where sovereignty is upheld by a class capable of posing a national project and of leading its implementation. In the peripheral capitalist societies, this question tends to take two forms: (a) the question of the possibility of the existence of a "national bourgeoisie" that bears a relatively autonomous national development project: and (b) the ethnic or peasant question (or the ethnopeasant question). Although the first refers more to the ability of the property-owning classes to lead a project that forms the nation based on their own particular interests, the second form refers to large sectors or

44

classes that are subordinated, whose subordinated integration or reproduction is counterposed to the alternative of its extinction (through homogenization, proletarianization, cultural integration, etc.).

In Nicaragua, the Sandinista People's Revolution changed the very content of the national question. Here the national question has to do mainly with the possibility of building, through a process of hegemony, a popular subject: the people, which are necessarily anti-imperialist, committed to world peace, an active participant in the defense of national sovereignty, and that proposes a project of national development and self-determined rearticulation within the world system, to society as a whole.

However, at the same time, the ethnic and peasant questions persist, only in different terms. It is no longer a matter of subordination/integration, but, rather because the question now lies in the very heart of the popular camp, it becomes an important aspect of the revolutionary subject. And also as a result of the revolution, what by analogy we could call the "bourgeois question" emerges.

THE "BOURGEOIS QUESTION"[28]

Even though the fact that the Nicaraguan economy interfaces with the world capitalist market implies that tendencies toward reproducing capitalist relations within the economy will operate, the following question is posed: Is it possible to achieve the subordinated reproduction of private capital when at the same time its bearers are alienated as a political class?

In the Sandinista People's Revolution's declared project and

---

28. The term *bourgeois* is used here to refer to the members of the capitalist class, bearers of a relationship that transcends them in that they must—due to capital's inherent logic and competition—make of accumulation their *primum-movile*. The conditions in which competition develops and the external mechanisms that capitalists may use for their individual growth have historically changed, and they change again when a revolution occurs. Therefore this does not prevent applying this term to the necessarily changed forms of capital, even though the "mode" no longer would be capitalist. The condition of being a private capitalist is accompanied in society by other factors, which are associated with the resulting inequality in the distribution of income—luxury spending. For the transition, both aspects are of interest: that of the possibility for private accumulation and that of privileged consumption.

45

effective practice, objective conditions are programmed so that private capital may reproduce itself, maintaining the ownership of the means of production, producing and distributing commodities, and obtaining profits that depend on the general situation of the economy but also on their competitive ability. However, the development of the inherent logic of capital would be hindered, first, because the global logic of the economy would not be governed by private accumulation but rather by meeting the needs of the population and national self-determination, and second, because private capital could not resort to state power to develop toward the form of finance capital nor to accumulate at the cost of the overexploitation of labor nor the centralization of other less competitive functions of capital.

Theoretically, this proposal is feasible, even though it must confront some conjunctural difficulties due to the present crisis the Central American economy is undergoing. For this matter, one must keep in mind that the Nicaraguan revolution is not proposing to exert control over "finance capital on a world scale" but rather the specific type of capital and capitalists it inherited.[29]

In economic terms, there should not be insurmountable problems for the capitalist class to subsist and reproduce itself, including on a larger scale. The real question is definitively political: Popular hegemony implies blocking—through hegemony's own means—the capitalist class' monopoly of state power. That is to say, this means blocking it from power as a class as such, which does not exclude the possibility that there may be members of the bourgeoisie (as there are now) in the government. This means obtaining the political alienation of the private capitalists—who

29. For example, in Nicaragua the term *cotton bourgeoisie* is used to refer to a particularly dynamic group of producers who applied modern technology and developed wage labor in the rural areas for the production of cotton. However, analysis demonstrates that the majority of these producers used rented land and machinery, require financing of up to 100 percent of their working capital and that many of them are absentee producers. If they suffer losses due to bad weather, the banks will usually refinance their debts. What kind of capitalists are these producers who do not risk their own capital? As for the medium-scale producers, their profits were usually spent on luxury goods or services—in Miami!

could not constitute a class-for-themselves and pretend to represent the national interest—not through coercion but rather through popular hegemony.

However, the social power of capital is never restricted to a predetermined "place" that could be held or taken by decree. Having nationalized foreign trade and the financial system, the revolution has expropriated capital's ability to accumulate on a social scale through centralization and monopoly as well as its ability to transnationalize itself. But the power of capital, even in a relatively unstructured society such as Nicaragua, is present in diverse institutions of society. As a result, national liberation requires a systematic dismantling of these relations and their substitution by or reintegration with others that have a popular character: in the factories, the farms, the schools, the family, and so forth. Only in this way—through a genuine and continuous cultural revolution—will the advance of popular hegemony undermine the base that capital still has to express itself politically.

In any case, the method that the Sandinista People's Revolution has put into practice implies—depending on the bourgeoisie's behavior—the possibility of the extinction of the class as such, but without traumata, in a process that could take several generations.

THE FORMATION OF A HEGEMONIC SUBJECT

The people/subject is not formed by aggregating "popular" sectors but rather by articulating them, through relationships defined by a project for liberation. This requires the recognition and slow resolution of several critical questions within the popular camp itself, which are normally considered secondary, such as the minority question within a multiethnic society, the peasant question, the liberation of women and of young people, and the recovery of the autochthonous elements of national culture without causing it to lose universality.

The identities of the people must be liberated. This does not imply that this liberation should not be accompanied by a profound transformation in that the forms that these identities have at present are also a product of a system of domination with which a rupture is being made.[30] And even more important, new identities will be developed. An example of this is the Sandinista Defense Committees that are an institutional expression not only of particular local identities but that are also fundamentally the expression of the establishment of social relations not mediated by the market such as community work to solve local problems or the defense of the community itself. All this permits the development of other forms of socialization, of self-management independent of the government apparatus, and of the exercise of democracy directly articulating the political with the economic.

In this process, new contradictions will emerge, and those already present will develop. In any case, these identities can only be realized if they are assumed by concrete and effective, that is, collectively organized, subjects. Along this line, the mass organizations must autonomously establish their particular objectives and goals in the struggle for liberation. It would be difficult to impose an outline of universal priorities or preestablished rhythms mapping the (necessarily unequal) advance of these identities from the outside.

The process of the formation of the people confronts powerful foreign and domestic forces and must even overcome the ideological barriers inherited from the system to be changed, which objectively tends to reproduce itself against the revolutionary will. In this sense, such autonomy is relative, in that the political situation indicates that the consolidation of power and the deactivation of the aggressor is fundamental for keeping open the possibility of liberation. As a consequence, the rhythm and content of the particular individual demands are collectively regulated with the strategic leadership provided by the FSLN, trying to link the specific struggles with (but not to reduce them to) the larger scale struggle against the imperialist system now taking place. The military struggle against imperialism is strengthened when the popular subject is consolidated in the struggle against other forms of domination in daily life, work, the family, and in the schools, guaranteeing at the same time mediating institutions for the globalization of these contradictions and their resolution in the popular project.

30. See Footnote 22.

The New Stage of Institutionalization and Its Prospects

THE 1984 MEASURES

From the beginning, the revolutionary government has made constant efforts toward institutionalizing new social relations, both on its own initiative and in response to demands made by various sectors. Even though the revolutionary government voided the Somocist constitution, all "residual law" remained untouched, in contrast with other revolutions where the totality of preexisting laws were annulled. In addition, the promulgation of the "Basic Statute" (July 20, 1979) and the "Statute regarding the Rights and Guarantees of Nicaraguans" (August 21, 1979) during the first weeks, together with around 1400 laws emitted during five years of revolutionary government clearly show that the "institutionalization" began on the very first day. On the other hand, a number of laws have been implemented in order to regulate situations of conflict (such as the right to property, the right to strike, the use of the mass media, the application of agrarian reform, etc.) as well as to form the expressly political institutions and their functions (the Council of State, the Political Parties Law, etc.). In fact, when the opposition minorities called for establishing the "rules of the game," what they really wanted was a different set of rules.

As was predicted in 1980, other important steps were taken toward the institutionalization of the new political system through the further formalization of political relationships in 1984. These forms—in that they could not be alien to pre- and post-triumph history—had to confirm the ideological, political, and economic pluralism of the revolutionary project but also reflect, as in all social systems, the correlation of forces that resulted after Somozas's overthrow. But beyond form, their very content and the subjects who implement them will also reflect the degree of development that the Nicaraguan people have achieved since 1979. Pluralism implies making it possible for the minorities to express themselves and make demands according to their particular interests, but its profoundly democratic character rests in the heart of the people itself, by allowing the expression of a social and ideological diversity that enriches the construction of a new society.

In this sense, in our opinion, the National Assembly formed

following the November 1984 elections might be just a (very important) moment of the constitutional stage of the new political system. Already, it would be very difficult—and in many aspects, a step backward given the experience obtained in the Council of State—to channel the differences within the people exclusively through a system of political parties, even if these fulfill the specific function of proposing wide-ranging alternatives for a popular and national project.

Thus it will be important to see how the revolution will, in time, resolve the limitations of representation exclusively on the basis of the political parties—limitations that are clearly seen in Europe where massive social movements overflow partisan channels when posing questions such as women's liberation, the need for stopping the arms race, the rational conservation of natural resources, and even class demands that cannot be fully represented by parties competing in a "homogeneous" field (the citizenry) for the votes needed to gain access to state power. Other forms of representation or direct participation of the identities of the people could then complement the partisan form.

In September 1983, the Political Parties Law was approved. It had been elaborated over several months of discussion in the Council of State and explicitly establishes that the political system include the principle of "the option to political power." The Election Law (approved on March 26, 1984) indicated that in the elections (which were announced for November 4, 1984), voters would choose a president, vice-president, and members of a ninety-member assembly. During its first two years of existence, the assembly was also to have a constituent character and later would keep only legislative functions. Politically, the only elements excluded from the electoral process were ex-officers of the National Guard and ex-members of the Somocist security force who had cases pending as well as those counterrevolutionary leaders who had called for foreign intervention, had solicited funds to fight against the revolution, or had directed or planned terrorist attacks.

With the goal of improving overall social conditions for this process—even under daily attack by terrorists and counterrevolutionaries financed and organized under the umbrella of "covert"

50

operations of the Reagan administration and the oligarchies allied with it in the region—the government proclaimed a general pardon for Miskito prisoners accused of counterrevolutionary activities as well as an amnesty benefitting those counterrevolutionaries who put down their weapons and returned to the country, with the exception of their leaders and those who had directed terrorist operations against Nicaragua. At the same time, diplomatic activities aimed at starting bilateral or multilateral negotiations were intensified, and support for the efforts carried out by the Contadora Group countries was reaffirmed.

The efficacy of these measures was evidenced by the reactions of the revolution's enemies: the Reagan administration, which had tried to justify its aggressive activities to the U.S. Congress by claiming that these actions were going to force the revolutionary government to "democratize" the country, began to argue that it did not believe the sincerity of the decision to hold the elections because "it was the result of fear." The most obstinate internal opposition that had been calling for "immediate elections" claimed that there was not enough time or presented conditions that it knew were unacceptable to a people that were proud to have expelled the imperialist guard from their country in the name of Sandino (they called for the elections to be "supervised" by foreign nations). The Honduran government blocked the visits by Nicaraguan missions to the counterrevolutionary camps and the Miskito concentration camps (where they were going to announce the mechanism of the amnesty), at the same time as it continued to offer its territory for the construction of a gigantic U.S. military base playing the same role that Somoza had played in the past.

THE CONTEXT OF THE NEW PHASE OF INSTITUTIONALIZATION

On the other hand, the external conditions under which the Nicaraguan people were preparing themselves to hold the first free elections in their history were very difficult. Without any immediate possibilities of resolving the foreign strangulation inherited from and accented by the boycott induced by the U.S. administration, the government was on the verge of implementing a program of macroeconomic adjustment that implied reducing the subsidies of basic consumer goods among other things and recognizing the impossibility of an immediate answer to urban unemployment together with an immediate additional reduction of the middle classes' spending on nonessential goods and services. At the same time, Nicaragua was to hold elections while at gunpoint because the Reagan administration had given no sign of withdrawing the Somocist Guard and even allocated more funds for covert and overt actions against Nicaragua in 1984. Even if, as some said, Reagan did not plan an invasion of Nicaragua "before his reelection," the fact was that the situation was increasingly tense and "all systems were go" for such an invasion. The probability of losing political control of those military systems was very high in a region in which the United States was allied with death squads, oligarchies, and paranoid military officers. Therefore, the Nicaraguan people did not have much room for speculation and had to stay alert against a possible invasion. This threat and the constant attacks from Honduran and Costa Rican territories and the counterrevolutionary organization's announcement that it was going to begin urban terrorist actions would justify any country's maintenance of a state of emergency that the counterrevolution's internal and foreign spokesmen criticized as "hardly favorable" for a climate for elections.

PROSPECTS FOR THE FUTURE

Even though very few doubt that, if there is not a U.S. invasion, the revolution will continue to consolidate itself, the institutionalization of an open electoral system that permits access to governmental power was seen by some of the Sandinista People's Revolution's friends as a potential danger for the survival of the revolutionary process. For those who see things in this way, the right wing's internal and foreign tools for ideological manipulation, the economy's enormous foreign dependence, and the U.S. administration's boycott—which tries to present a real alternative for power from outside the country—could create a situation in 1990 in which the bourgeoisie would win consensus for displacing the revolutionary representatives through elections.

However, this catastrophic vision would seem to suppose that nothing has changed in Nicaraguan civil society nor in the nature of the state. It implies assuming that the opposition bourgeoisie that is backward and lacks a national project would be dealing with the same popular masses as in the past who are unorganized, politically inexperienced, alienated from social management, lacking an understanding of the structural processes that determine their living conditions, without a praxis of struggle, and lacking consciousness of their own identity as the people and as the conscious subject of national sovereignty. It also supposes returning to a situation in which the masses found themselves facing an apparatus characterized by repression, terror, and the limitation of their individual and social rights, all of which made elections a farce. But this was the situation in the Somocist past. The sociopolitical context has been drastically transformed by the FSLN's long struggle, the mass insurrection, and, later, by the consolidation of revolutionary power.

Besides, we must not forget the nature of the most obstinate opposition. An objective analysis of events starting in 1977 shows that many of those who now oppose the Sandinista People's Revolution and claim to feel "betrayed" because they played a role in Somoza's overthrow only entered into the massive front against Somoza during the final days. In addition, many of these are the same people who were trying to negotiate with the U.S. government up to the last moment to achieve "Somocism without Somoza," maintaining the National Guard after cleaning its ranks of the most obvious assassins that formed it. On the other hand, the opposition as a whole is incapable of presenting an alternative, meaningful national project to the Nicaraguan people because it has remained ideologically dependent on the United States, to the extreme that at present, it is the Reagan administration and its Somocist guard now based in Honduras that is trying to create a true alternative—although exclusively through the military route—to popular power in Nicaragua.

It would be naive to believe that, without foreign pressure and material difficulties and with international solidarity respectful of the right of the Nicaraguan people to choose their own destiny, the Sandinista People's Revolution would find itself faced with an easy road to continue this process that is seen by many as a "wonderful experiment of humanity." The only real historical path for building a new society is through permanent struggle.

53

In any case, a notable fact of the Nicaraguan people and their revolutionary leadership is that they have developed the ability to turn the enemy's own forces against themselves. The failure of the desperate attempts by imperialism and its weak internal allies to use the elections as a Trojan horse and the institutionalization as a break in the process of social revolution are other examples of the dialectical relationship between the revolution and those who seek to restore a social system of domination of the majority by a minority, guided by the logic of capitalism.

In the same way that the Sandinista People's Revolution has learned from the struggles of other peoples, others may learn from this fresh and unique revolutionary method of building a pluralist, sovereign people that is bent on building a new, just, and self-determined society that is committed to peace. The revolutionary project has been forged in the daily dialectic of the struggle and, in this sense, it would be a mistake to try to pigeonhole it in a predetermined, rigid model of one kind or another. What we have tried to show here is that a true possibility exists in the Sandinista People's Revolution for developing a creative alternative to what should never be presented as a dichotomy: *Democracy and revolution have always been the banners of Sandino's people.*

Epilogue: A Note Concerning Methodology

If it is difficult in general to analyze and interpret aspects of a society undergoing a process of reproduction, it is even more difficult to try doing so for a society in the process of revolutionizing its structures, in the moment in which still undefined forms begin to emerge and characteristics of the society it is trying to overcome are openly or covertly reproduced.

The very absence of global theories about transition creates additional difficulties. One runs the risk of falling into empiricism: In view of the lack of a theory, we could provisionally present the semichaotic elapse of transition as a continuum of events registered and systematized by "themes" derived from other social theories. The application of predetermined values about what is socially or politically correct allows us to show how many "positive" things occur during transition and how many "negative" things occur at the same time. The temptation to "describe"—without evaluating—is great, given the high risk of incorrectly interpreting the totality of certain "events" when the reality continues to be the superposition of inherited contradictions on top of new contradictions and when all of society's elements are undergoing an intensive transformation/reaccommodation to a greater or lesser degree.

A relatively "simple" alternative is to substitute the *imposition of an ideological model* of what a revolution should be. The followers of a given ideological line will seek out (and generally find) traits and data that support the idea that the revolution finally corresponds to a particular characterization within a predetermined system of classification.

A third possibility—which is what I have tried to implement here—is to *theorize* about the revolution as a complex flux in which the revolution-to-be is unfolded through the development of multiple contradictions. This revolution can be seen in the form of actual tendencies, at times led by concrete and conscious subject-agents who push for a global revolutionary project, at times through blind processes resulting from the social interaction of particular or sectorial projects. But the possibility arises here that the interpretation of the nature of the revolution is tied to the type of abstraction made in the analysis.

According to which elements and traits are highlighted, a specific characterization of the revolution will emerge. As I said earlier, in the semichaos and semiorder of transition, it is possible to see various revolutions, all of which are convincing if one abides to the facts presented to illustrate the analysis. Here ideology plays a fundamental role because one tends to see or give importance to what one considers to be "positive" or "negative," according to one's own point of view.

How then can the nature of Nicaragua's transition be "scientifically" and objectively evaluated? Our objectivity consists of recognizing the limitations of what we have presented. I have presented "one" of the revolutions, existing as a complex effective global tendency in the present historical development of Nicaragua. This profoundly democratic and just revolution has tried to concretize itself in the midst of a network of internal and foreign forces that, consciously in some cases and unconsciously in others, fight for a "project" of a new society. A complete analysis would require presenting the "other" revolutions that could result from this epoch of Nicaraguan history. It would be useless to also present the possible return to the status quo on which powerful foreign forces are bent. But I have not attempted to do so because I know that I am presenting the partial results of an analytical work that should be collective and therefore, does not require that every contribution be formally complete. In addition, I feel that this is the revolution that presents a new alternative for socialist revolution in Latin America and the world and, for that reason, should be highlighted.

Another guard against our falling into subjectivity is that I do not attempt to find the keys for establishing the nature of the revolution in the statements made by its leaders. This analysis is fundamental, but it also is the most common. I feel that, given the pragmatism demonstrated by Nicaragua's revolutionary leaders in such a fluid situation, where the changing conjunctural situation generates changing specific responses, it would be possible to find contradictions in their discourse that, over time, would be nothing more than a reflection of this dialectical relationship between the subject and the process and between the project and reality. What interests us more is the reconstruction of the project-in-action that materializes from within the process itself, beyond the realm of discourse. At the same time, this leads to the depersonalization of the revolution, posing precisely the question of the revolutionary subject and its constitutive process.

Chapter 3

Social Movements and Revolution: The Case of Nicaragua

Theorizing about Social Movements and Social Struggle

The decade of the 1960s witnessed the emergence of new ideas about social struggle. These ideas were inspired by the new organizational practices and forms of development adopted by social forces in Europe and the United States. These forces or "social movements," as they are usually called, are organized around specific demands (housing, urban services, women's liberation, environmental conservation, the antinuclear struggle, etc.). In many cases, these movements are engaged in a struggle with state institutions; sometimes, however, their actions are directed at other types of organizations.

The multiclass nature of these movements, their ability to mobilize large numbers of people plus the fact that their demands were acquiring a radical character—and therefore could not be met without a profound transformation of the existing social system—all attracted the attention of political parties and social theorists alike.

The political parties saw a challenge that consisted of trying to articulate, strengthen, and regulate these forces in line with the traditional forms of political struggle. The theorists were faced with the need to understand the consequences of these developments on political theory, in particular, on theories of a revolutionary character that claimed to provide a scientific basis for the practice of social transformation. In some cases, pressing political circumstances led researchers to reach theoretically questionable conclusions, based perhaps more on ideological predispositions than on scientific analysis.[1]

In both instances, the fact that social movements became fashionable led to their "proliferation" at the conceptual level. Classification systems were developed, and various attributes of given sectors (according to gender, age, territorial situation, consumption of particular goods, ethnic identity, nationality, tax status, etc.) were measured and categorized in order to permit speculation about their "agitational or antisystem potential." Simultaneously, these ideas together with their corresponding political practices spread to other continents, particularly to Latin America where in some situations—by no means in all of them—they were in line with local developments.[2]

This process can be characterized as an analytical moment when societies are "pulverized"—in conceptual as well as organizational terms—into these simple determinations found in a variety of social contradictions. However, just as theoretical analyzation represents a failure of scientific practice if the movement toward synthesis and reconstruction of the object is not completed, so practical-organizational analyzation rapidly leads to a waste of energy and loses effectiveness in the absence of a conjunctural accumulation of social forces able to effectively challenge the existing system.

From this perspective, it becomes theoretically necessary, on the one hand, to reconstruct the concept of "the people" as a synthesis (articulation) of a multiplicity of determinations. On the other hand, it becomes politically necessary to critically reconsider the role of the revolutionary party as the articulator (synthesizer)

1. See the pioneering work of Manuel Castells and J. Lojkine on urban social movements and their "explication" on the basis of the concepts of reproduction of the labor force or of the general conditions of production.

2. In fact, some theoreticians find it meaningful to ask themselves whether Sendero Luminoso in Peru is a "social movement." See David Slater, ed., *New Social Movements and the State in Latin America* (Amsterdam: CEDLA, 1985), where this essay was included.

of the various social forces that demonstrate a potential for action directed against the system.

The usual characterization of the "people" as a social class with a theoretically predetermined "historical destiny" and the assignment of the role of *subject* to a particular party—seen as the vehicle of this "objective consciousness"—could be criticized in a way that brings new elements to the discussion of the social revolution. Nevertheless, as long as the "problem of the people" continues to be seen as a mere question of conceptual definition, separate from the real problem of the vanguard's self-perpetuation, our progress would remain limited. It should also be said that the transitional need for a vanguard cannot be put into question without falling into the trap of spontaneity.

In our opinion, a real break takes place when the concept of "the people" is redefined in terms of identity and organizational factors and when this is coupled with the idea of a complex subject that constitutes neither a class, a party, nor a movement but rather a hegemonic system.[3] Here the concept of "the people" is no longer derived from what is basically an economicist theory of the inevitable tendencies of capitalist society that, in any case, would be accelerated by the actions of the vanguards. On the contrary, the concrete contradictions that run through the state and civil society and the differential positions of the social agents in material, ideological or organizational terms will provide the "objective" basis for an analysis that—from the perspective of power relations—will make it possible to develop a strategy of popular hegemony. The primacy of the political in relation to revolutionary

3. See Ernesto Laclau, "Socialisme et transformation des logiques hégémoniques" and Chantal Mouffe, "Socialisme, democratie et nouveaux mouvements sociauz." In *La gauche, le pouvoir, le socialisme*, ed. C. Buci-Glucksman (Paris: PUF, 1983); Laclau and Mouffe, "Socialist Strategy—Where Next?", *Marxism Today* (January 1981); and Bob Jessop, "The Political Indeterminancy of Democracy." In *Marxism and Democracy*, ed. A. Hunt. In fact, the problematic of social movements is closely related to the critique of "real socialism" and "real democracy" as well as with the current that sees the struggle for democracy in Latin America as a popular, not necessarily a bourgeois, struggle.

practice does not make it any less necessary—quite the contrary—to take account of class oppositions and to move toward an eventual theoretical reconstruction of economic laws and their historical tendencies.

By observing practice as such, we see the impossibility of establishing a one-to-one correspondence between concrete agents and specific identities (determined by gender, class, age, ethnic identity, etc.). Given that the diverse contradictions underlying these identities do not necessarily converge, neither in a single individual agent or organization nor at the level of the people as a whole, it becomes impossible to reduce the identification of the "popular" to a single determination. At the same time, an effective hegemonic practice does not presuppose a given complex subject but sets out to constitute it as the people. This, in turn, requires the elaboration of an articulated discourse, the popular project, that concretely makes explicit the content of the new society yet to be constructed. Far from being a utopia, the popular project is a viable proposal for a struggle waged in solidarity against an oppressive system, where the effectiveness of action and possible outcomes can be predicted and where conjunctural analysis and perspective allow popular ideologies to advance. This must take place in a climate of respect for existing autonomies and identities where there is a simultaneous rearticulation and development of these same identities.

Moreover, insofar as power relations are not reduced to relations "between" the state and civil society but are seen to be present in various instances and institutions of society as a whole, the people's project for liberation cannot be reduced to the idea of a given oppositional social entity "seizing" governmental power. Instead, it presupposes a permanent revolution of civil society and therefore a continuous transformation of the subject, that is, the people.

Here I shall attempt to discuss the question of whether the perspective described so far can have universal applications, basing the discussion on the experience of the Sandinista People's Revolution, some of whose specific features are described later. Then, toward the end of this chapter, I shall return to the theoretical problematic.

The Practice of Social Transformation in Nicaragua

Armed Struggle, Counterhegemonic Practice, and Nicaragua

Popular insurrection—involving a breakdown of the economic system, a permanent state of siege directed at the enemy, and the coming together of all the identities of a population to rise up against an oppressive regime—represents an instant in the history of the constitution of a people. Specifically, it is a moment when contradictions are condensed and social forces have but a single objective—the overthrow of a regime.

In Nicaragua, this moment would not have arrived in 1979 had it not been for the long-standing presence of the Sandinista National Liberation Front on the political scene. Its very survival as a guerrilla force, through good and bad times, served as a constant reminder of the possibility of challenging the Somoza regime. However, its organic ties with the masses only became fully developed during the two years before its triumph. Until then, the FSLN carried out military actions on the one hand and partial counterhegemonic practices on the other, participating in the organization of students, women, workers, and neighborhoods in what could be called a passive accumulation of forces.[4] "The accumula-

4. See Humberto Ortego Saavedra, *Sobre la insurrección* (Havana: Ed. de Ciencias Sociales, 1981). On the origins of the mass organizations associated with the FSLN before the triumph, see CIERA, *La democracia participativa en Nicaragua* (Managua: May 1984). Certain organizations were under the FSLN's direct control. In the trade union area, they were the Trade Union Movement of the Working People (MSPT), the Revolutionary Workers' Committees (COR), and the Committee for Workers' Struggle (CLT) in the urban areas. The Committee of Rural Workers initially organized in 1977 and was composed of workers, semiproletarians, and small agricultural producers; it was later to become the Asociación de Trabajadores del Campo (ATC—Rural Workers' Association). Within the student movement, these organizations included the Revolutionary Student Front, the Revolutionary Christian Movement, the Sandinista Revolutionary Youth, the School Students' Movement, the Association of Secondary School Students, and the Managua Federation of Youth Movements. At the neighborhood level, the FSLN called for setting up the Civil Defense Committees (CDC) that were to play a crucial role during the insurrection. Also in 1977, the Association of Women Concerned with the National Problematic (AMPRONAC), clearly directed by the FSLN, was created.

tion of forces is only possible in specific conjunctural situations; otherwise, it cannot take place."[5] The strategy of insurrection implies that organization no longer precedes action because the challenge to all the institutions that reproduce the repressive system is simultaneous, involving unequal forces while growing as events unfold, establishing spontaneous solidarity against a common enemy, one that is so obvious that there is no need to unmask or decode it. Doubtless proof of the FSLN's qualifications as vanguard was evidenced by its ability to reveal the regime's repressive and exploitative nature, thus dooming to failure any attempt to camouflage or reform it and to demonstrate its political and military vulnerability. However, once within the context of the insurrection, the FSLN often followed and acted in support of the masses rather than the opposite.[6]

Even if the FSLN were to have had a more global vision of the secondary contradictions and their possible articulation, at the moment of insurrection the various identities of the people came together, and their common goal predominated: to destroy the regime and its various political and military agents. The popular organizations have served more as a network of communication than as a channel for conducting specific struggles. Even though organizations with specific demands conducting the struggle in particular ways were born, this was not a universal phenomenon, and in any event, they tended to vary according to the conjunctural situation. For example, the principal demands underlying the struggle of the Asociación de Mujeres ante la Problemática Nacional (AMPRONAC—Association of Women Concerned about the National Problematic) were more related to the question of human rights, disappeared persons, and support for the mothers of victims of the National Guard than with typical feminist demands. Again, although students and workers did organize within their schools, universities, and workplaces, as the struggle developed, unemployment increased dramatically and schools were closed. Students and workers then began organizing in their neighborhoods and the Comités de Defensa Sandinista (CDS—Sandinista

5. Humberto Ortega Saavedra, *Sobre la insurrección.*
6. *Ibid.*

Defense Committees) benefited from this additional organizational experience that served to supplement the neighborhoods' existing organizational base. In fact, the various mass organizations did not so much affirm and defend specific interests on the basis of their particular identities, but rather they used these identities as a means of mobilizing social forces for a frontal struggle against the Somoza regime. A fundamental role of the student organizations, therefore, was to provide cadres for the rural guerrilla struggle.

Thus a momentary universalization takes place: a massification of the people in contradiction with the attempt to organize specific social movements and to salvage their individual demands. This phenomenon was to continue after the triumph in some cases—as that of the Asociación de Mujeres Nicaragüeneses "Luisa Amanda Espinoza" (AMNLAE—Luisa Amanda Espinoza Nicaraguan Women's Association)—leading to differences in perspective between the Nicaraguan organizations and equivalent organizations abroad.[7] Moreover, the FSLN reached the moment of triumph with the people at the center of a broad anti-Somocist front, which would apparently imply a fading out of the class content of the revolutionary project. Nevertheless, the concrete conditions of the triumph, involving the complete dismantling of the National Guard and the creation of the Sandinista People's Army as well as unceasing efforts to consolidate the popular organizations were to ensure the defeat of an emergency project articulated by the financial bourgeoisie designed to convert itself into a hegemonic or "dictatorial" force "without Somoza."[8] At the same time, by ensuring the unity of a broad range of social forces struggling against Somocism and its substitutes—supported until the last moment by the U.S. administration—the FSLN succeeded in neutralizing the imperialist project in all of its variants, in such a

7. See Maxime Molyneux, "Mobilization without Emancipation? Women's Interests, State and Revolution in Nicaragua." In *New Social Movements*.

8. See *Nicaragua: la estrategia de la victoria* (Mexico: Ed. Nuestro Tiempo, 1980). See also Amalia Chamorro Z., *Algunos rasgos hegemónicos del Somocismo y la Revolución Sandinista*, Cuadernos de Pensamiento Propio [Managua], Essay Series 5 (June 1983).

way as to ensure that the class content of the revolution could not be put into question on the basis of the characteristics of that social configuration at the moment of the triumph.

Popular Hegemony as Revolutionary Practice

The experience of the Popular Unity government in Chile is often cited to support the thesis that it is impossible to "have power" if the control of the government administrative structures is not coupled with control of the repressive apparatus. According to this vision, the revolutionary forces in Nicaragua have indeed "taken power." The difficulty is that this vision is based on a rather limited definition of power that is seen to reside in a particular state apparatus.

This vision, which makes a sharp distinction between political and civil society and which views power relations as belonging to the sphere of the former (and between it and civil society), has been criticized by those who point to the political content of relations that take place inside various institutions of society (the factory, the school, the family, the church, corporative organizations, etc.). Again, according to this view, far from having achieved popular power, the triumphant revolution against the Somocist regime is only now beginning to build this power. The slow dismantling of the inherited power relations had to be carried out simultaneously with the construction of a new system of social power. As long as this is not achieved, the old relations will tend to be reproduced and with them the corresponding ideology of domination within the revolutionary process. From this perspective, the process of building popular power implies that the masses must negate their own existence through a process of organization, of self-trans-formation, of developing their identities and creating new identities while others disappear. Having been "massified" by generations of repression and ideological domination, the masses also carry identities that must be overcome and transformed (racism, machismo, authoritarianism, and individualism are not qualities exclusive to the dominant classes).

Although the FSLN was again to play a fundamental role in this process, the masses with their incipient organizations and their daily struggles would continue to have the same kind of changing dialectical relations with the vanguard as before the triumph: at times, under the guidance of the FSLN; at other times, ahead of and autonomous from it; and generally without a neatly defined formula defining the relationship between revolutionary party and mass organization. And in this process, both terms of the relationship between the mass organizations and the revolutionary party were to undergo modifications in form as well as content.

Just as prior to the insurrection, the role of the FSLN was to point out the strategic objective. In this case, the objective was to build a new society based on the negation of the global logic of capital, ensuring that the imperatives of social accumulation remained subordinate to the satisfaction of the population's basic needs, achieving an effective democracy, popular sovereignty, and national self-determination. At the same time, it was to indicate the immediate priority task—the consolidation of revolutionary power that was necessary to confront external and internal enemies and leave open the possibility of transforming society. However, within this broad orientation, the increasingly organized masses were to put forward their own answers, thus enriching and giving concrete content to the revolutionary project and translating the idea of popular power into reality. This, in turn, was to produce changes in the very structure of the revolutionary party.

This task required certain material conditions as well as a political-ideological framework. Through oral and written discourse, but more fundamentally through its actions, the FSLN showed the political nature of the revolution: This was not the path leading to the "dictatorship of the proletariat"—the nationalization of the means of production and a single party system—but another road leading to "popular hegemony." But this was a hegemony to be constructed along with the historical subject of the revolution—the Nicaraguan people. Rather than moving toward the homogenization of the popular sectors, differences were acknowledged and indeed reflected within the various mass organizations and their principal liberating demands (the peasantry, rural and urban salaried workers, women, youth, indigenous communities). At the same time, a new identity was consolidated

65

whose embryonic form is found in anti-Somocist struggles—the Sandinista Defense Committees. The CDS represent the possibility of self-government, of direct social relations in community work, without mercantile mediations.[9]

THE YOUTH

The accumulation of forces is only possible in particular conjunctural situations. The revolution presents tasks that are assumed by the masses, though not without contradictions. Throughout this process, new identities are created, and others that lay dormant and oppressed are transformed and liberated. For example, the literacy campaign gave great social influence to the July 19 Sandinista Youth Organization as a political organization under the direction of the FSLN, through a process that transformed the traditional relations between city and country, family relations, and relations in the educational centers. The resistance from the Right that developed in the wake of the National Literacy Campaign led to an accumulation of this new social force. In the same way, new identities began to emerge. The popular teachers (there are 19,000 volunteer educators in Nicaragua) —the fundamental subjects of the postliteracy period—demonstrate the possibility, when necessary, of breaking with professionalism and the educational monopoly while showing the people's capacity for innovation and autonomous action in relation to the state apparatus.

MUNICIPAL GOVERNMENT

When the people had to take charge of local government, the new Municipal Reconstruction Councils provided another example of this process of discovering the capacity of the people to govern themselves. After the triumph, 136 municipalities previously under the control of local *caudillos* or representatives of local economic interests were taken over by agricultural workers,

9. The Sandinista Defense Committees have performed such tasks as organizing the supply of rationed products and night watch duties. Originating from the CDC, they now have approximately 600,000 members and are purported to be both a multiclass and nonpartisan organization.

peasants, or urban workers, many of whom did not even have a primary-school education.[10]

THE MILITIA

The task of defending the revolution has given rise to the Sandinista People's Militia, which is probably the best example of the same process, though one that cannot be appreciated by those who continue to see power as residing by definition in certain parts of the state apparatus. The transfer and subsequent consolidation of the masses' ability to wage combat was not limited to weekly training sessions but involved actual battles against the counter-revolutionaries who were constantly infiltrating into the country from Honduras. In fact, during an early phase, the fight against the Somocists—supported by the Reagan administration and the Central American oligarchies—was conducted mainly by the militias and not by the Sandinista People's Army. An organized people learned how to defend itself, first by organizing extraterritorial battalions, then by setting up territorial militias, again breaking a professional monopoly that the capitalist state guards jealously.[11]

THE PEASANTS

In other cases, it is clear how the revolutionary context made it possible for a previously oppressed and alienated identity to become qualitatively transformed and come to play a crucial role in the revolutionary process. Under Somocism, Nicaraguan peasants were not permitted to organize in defense of their interests. Until late 1980, one year after the triumph, their interests were still being "represented" by agricultural corporations controlled by large producers. In December 1980, the small producers of the Department of Matagalpa decided to break with the Central Cooperative of Coffee Producers and to form the Provisional Committee

10. See Charles Downs and Fernando Kusnetzoff, "The Changing Role of Local Government in the Nicaraguan Revolution," *International Journal of Urban and Regional Research* 6, no. 4 (1982): 533–48.

11. The 1983 Law on Patriotic Military Service resulted in further socializing the task of national defense, thus breaking down the bias that the Sandinista People's Army was made up primarily of people coming from the lower income sectors.

of Small and Medium Producers to encourage small producers in other departments to meet. These meetings provided the impetus for the formation of the National Farmers and Cattlemen's Union (UNAG). Not only did UNAG immediately begin to present economic demands to the government, it also asked to be represented in the Council of State and in various bodies dealing with the problems facing the agricultural sector. From then on, this mass organization has gained increasing political space, maintaining a critical attitude to what are considered to be deviations from the policy of agrarian reform and its content. During the first year of the revolution, there was a discussion of the emphasis that would have to be made either on the cooperative model or on a statist management model based on socialization of the productive forces. The development of a peasant identity made possible and encouraged by the revolutionary process will have an impact on agrarian strategy to the year 2000. Both models of socialization would be implemented in a parallel and complementary fashion.[12] However, the combination of production and defense as a result of increasing foreign aggression has given UNAG an enormous impulse and set it firmly at the center of the revolutionary process. The agrarian reform benefiting the peasantry is being accelerated beyond what simple technical criteria would admit. Peasants are demanding and being given both land and arms, and this is taking place within an irreversible process of class consolidation in the context of an authentic social and political revolution.[13]

In July 1984, UNAG took another step that consolidated its position as a significant social force within the revolutionary process. It decided to incorporate agricultural producers regardless of the size of their holdings, with the only condition that they should productively support the process of national liberation.[14] In other

12. See *Estrategia de desarrollo agropecuario y reforma agraria* (Managua: MIDINRA, December 1982).

13. The most explicit forms that this phenomenon has taken are the almost 200 Defense and Production Cooperatives, with almost 7000 members in the border areas.

14. See the statements by Daniel Núñez in *Barricada* (official organ of the FSLN), 7 July 1984, and the announcement made at the Second Assembly of UNAG, published in *Barricada*, 9 July 1984.

situations, such a measure would have undoubtedly led to a situation where a few large landowners came to dominate the mass of small producers and then use the organization for their own benefit. In the context of a social revolution, however, it implies the reverse: Popular hegemony presupposes the integration of the minorities under the leadership of the majorities.

WOMEN

The case of the Luisa Amanda Espinoza Nicaraguan Women's Association is a different one. This organization has been especially active whenever issues concerning women were being discussed, such as the law on the family, or more recently, the law on patriotic military service that made service optional for women. In general, however, the association has not enjoyed the kind of increasing political influence that the European feminist movements in particular had hoped for and expected. This can be attributed to the greater difficulties involved in breaking down the ideological and material structures that perpetuate women's subordination in comparison with demands voiced by the youth and workers' organizations. However, as the leaders of AMNLAE have themselves stated, their priority task is to contribute by other means to the defense of the revolution, which is a necessary condition for the subsequent struggle for women's liberation.[15]

THE CONJUNCTURAL SITUATION AND THE DEVELOPMENT OF IDENTITIES

To be sure, the government—in this case, a revolutionary government—is in a position to regulate, block, or promote demands voiced by various sectors. However, our thesis is that the conjunctural situation, through a dialectical relation between revolutionary party and mass organizations, determines which identities will be developed, at what speed, and in which direction. The advance of the peasant sector can be explained in terms of the fact that their specific demands coincide with the material and ideological needs of the revolution (opening a real alternative for capitalist sectors that are reluctant to produce, placing restraints on the state bu-

15. See Molyneux, "Mobilization without Emancipation?"

reaucracy, developing production, and consolidating defense against foreign invasions).

In the case of the specific demands put forward by women, on the other hand, a new and complex area of struggle would have been opened up, not only against the opposition forces such as the church hierarchy but also within the popular front. The party is aware of this, and the women's organization itself is prepared to voice only limited demands while waiting for more favorable circumstances to develop when the "general interest" will no longer clash with the particular interests. Thus there is nothing structural about the revolutionary project that is likely to prevent the full liberation of Nicaraguan women.

THE CATHOLIC CHURCH

One mass organization that is not generally regarded as such is the Catholic church. It also corresponds to a deeply rooted identity of the Nicaraguan people. What I shall have to say about the Church also applies to other mass organizations. Pluralism and democracy are not matters relative to the way various organizations are externally linked. They also have something to do with what happens inside these organizations. In the case of the church, it is an institution that obviously existed before the revolution and that, in principle, is governed internally in accordance with strict rules of hierarchy. In fact, it would be difficult to imagine a more vertically oriented organization than the Catholic Church. However, in practice, there is a certain degree of pluralism within the Church, and different currents representing "secondary" contradictions within Christian thought coexist. In the context of a country struggling against imperialism, these come to assume great significance for the conjunctural situation of the Church. With a Catholic population engaged in a process of liberation ready to fight to the death against its oppressors, the internal equilibrium of the Catholic hierarchy cannot be discussed out of context without risking alienating its own popular base.

In reality, although the highest authority of the Church states explicitly that it disagrees with the development of the revolution, the Christian and revolutionary identities have entered into a special relationship, to the point where several obviously Christian

70

principles have been incorporated as revolutionary ideology by the FSLN. At the same time, many priests and many of the faithful are prepared to challenge the counterrevolutionary political guidance given to them by their own hierarchy without abandoning their apostolic mission or their Christian faith. The counterrevolution has tried every means possible to break this unity and to use the Church as the ideological platform that the weak bourgeois opposition is unable to provide.[16] Paradoxically, it is the FSLN that is involved in preserving the unity of Christianity and the revolution and that sees no contradictions between the two.

THE ETHNIC MINORITIES

The clearest evidence that the identities of the masses do not automatically develop in a way that contributes to the consolidation of the revolution is offered by the case of the indigenous communities (Miskitos, Sumus, and Ramas) and the Creoles of the Atlantic coast. In 1981, the FSLN and the government issued a statement of principles in which they committed themselves to support the maintenance of indigenous cultural traditions; to guarantee participation in the affairs of the nation (the Misurasata organization immediately took its place within the Council of State), and in those of the Atlantic coast, in particular, to provide legal guarantees of ownership of their land holdings—either as communal lands or in the form of cooperatives; and to "support the organizational forms coming from the communities themselves in order to achieve the necessary degree of representation in the social, political, and economic institutions that direct the affairs of the Atlantic zone."[17] However, these principles were not taken to heart by a community whose relations with the state had always been marginal, whose dealings with multinational corporations had led to exploitation and loss of resources, and who were used to viewing the inhabitants of the rest of the country as "Spaniards."

16. See Ana María Ezcurra, *Agresión ideológica contra la Revolución Sandinista* (Mexico: Ediciones Nuevomar, 1983).

17. See *Declaraciones de principios de la Revolución Popular Sandinista sobre las comunidades indígenas de la Costa Atlántica*, CIERA, *La Democracia participativa*, p. 156.

Another negative inheritance from the past was the fact that their participation in the struggle against Somoza had been marginal. Moreover, a revolutionary transformation of the indigenous identity implied not only a change in the way the communities articulated with the outside world but also a change in outlook on the part of the revolutionary forces—something that is very difficult to achieve when judged by the long series of unsuccessful attempts to deal with the ethnic question, not only in Latin America but in other parts of the world. The fact that the Contras infiltrated into the Atlantic zone at the same time as certain communities' religious leaders began to identify the revolution with "the devil" gave rise to situations in which the response of the FSLN or the government cannot always be seen as an "error." In many cases, this response was the inevitable result of the real contradiction between the need to defend territorial integrity against external aggression and the desire to allow self-determination and a gradual rearticulation of the indigenous communities with the society-in-revolution.[18] The case of the indigenous communities illustrates that the process of liberation of identities requires a transformation of relations (in this case interethnic) by both parties and that evolution is not exclusively dependent upon the decisions of a government or a revolutionary party.

THE WORKING CLASS

One area in which the FSLN has played an important role in placing limits on the "natural" development of a popular identity is that of the salaried workers. The economic difficulties inherited from the past as well as those that emerged as a result of a deterioration in the terms of trade and a rise in interest rates, the obvious weaknesses of a state that is being constructed, natural disasters, and the economic and financial boycott imposed by the Reagan administration plus the political decision to maintain a broad internal front under popular hegemony required that certain

18. For an objective report on this problem, see *"Trabil Nani," History and Current Situation in Nicaragua's Atlantic Coast* (Managua: CIDCA, 1984). A summarized version is available in *ENVIO* 3, no. 36 (June 1984) (*ENVIO* is published by the Instituto Histórico Centroamericano, located in Managua).

forms of the class struggle had to be slowed down. These forms included the old economic demands by the trade unions that had been suppressed before the revolution and a generalized demand for workers' control over the means of production. The limits placed on the forms of struggle were also applied to land occupations by the peasantry.[19]

The decision to opt for popular hegemony implied the maintenance of a pluralist social system that, in turn, had to accommodate the demands of private proprietors for property guarantees and for the chance to make a profit without being stigmatized as exploiters. The revolutionary government provided these guarantees on the condition that private property fulfill its social function: to produce under acceptable conditions of efficiency.[20]

Thus the class struggle was not arrested; it simply took other forms—workers' control over the use of property,[21] demands for improved working conditions, demands for an indirect salary from the state, and, fundamentally, something the workers' organizations still had to delegate to parts of the government apparatus, control of the economic surplus through economic policy as well as through the state monopoly of both the financial system and the marketing of major products. This new expression of workers' identity required an understanding of the conjunctural situation

19. On November 21, 1979, the FSLN issued a communique ordering "the immediate and complete suspension of all confiscations and interventions of residences, vehicles, and rural and urban properties" (see *Barricada* of that day). Through the Sandinista Workers' Central (CST) and the Rural Workers' Association (ATC), the FSLN impressed upon the population that it was necessary to maintain production levels. However, in the face of foreign aggression that was already on the rise, the revolutionary government had to resort to the Law of Social and Economic State of Emergency (Decree No. 812) of September 9, 1981, which penalized land invasions and the occupation of workplaces and strikes. See *Leyes de la República de Nicaragua*, vol. 5 (Managua: Ministerio de Justicia, July–December 1981).

20. See the Law of Agrarian Reform (Decree No. 782, August 10, 1981) that was characterized as "productivist" by critics belonging to the extreme Left. In *Leyes de la República*, vol. 5.

21. The Law on Decapitalization (Decree No. 805, August 28, 1981) was going to allow workers to maintain strict vigilance over the management of private capital in this area.

and a clarity regarding the revolutionary project that not all workers possessed. The situation was worsened by the general crisis of the Central American industrial sector that also affected Nicaragua and slowed down the planned expansion of urban employment. Therefore, it is not surprising that the government had to resort to legal measures in order to suppress certain strikes, given the emergency conditions affecting the country, even though the principle of trade union pluralism had allowed the survival of certain trade unions that tended to voice classical demands as well as that of certain opposition unions that were now waving banners they had never raised during the Somoza dictatorship.[22]

In the absence of seasonal migratory movements from abroad and thanks to unprecedented levels of coffee production and a recovery in cotton production, rural workers were in a position to achieve some of their traditional demands (improved working conditions, a social wage, fair pay for work done, etc.) and even to place limits on the progress of mechanization of the cotton harvest whenever labor power was available. The identity of the rural workers as proletarians was maintained, and the possibility of a movement rushing back to the land (the reconstitution of the peasantry) was not effective. One thing that did affect the short-term availability of labor power was foreign aggression, not only because it gave rise to a strong migratory movement toward the cities but also because it resulted in the mobilization of workers as soldiers and militia members for the purpose of defending the country. These labor shortages were constantly being met through voluntary work.[23] Given the importance of the Areas de Propiedad del Pueblo (APP—People's Property) for permanent rural employment, one of the increasingly widespread demands was for effective worker par-

22. In fact, the trade unions multiplied after the revolutionary triumph. From 133 trade unions with 27,000 members, numbers rose by December 1983 to 1103 trade unions with 207,391 members, of which approximately 80 percent accept the leadership of the FSLN. See CIERA, *La Democracia participativa*, p. 45.

23. Approximately 40,000 volunteer workers participated in the 1983–1984 coffee and cotton harvest, thus constituting a new identity of the Nicaraguan people. See CIERA. *ibid.*, pp. 64–65.

ticipation, which gave rise to a contradiction with the bureau-cratic tendencies of certain government officials.[24]

THE LANDLORDS

The construction of popular hegemony presupposes not only the development but also the articulation of the identities of the people as the subject of the revolution. Moreover, and in contradic-tion to this, it also involves the reproduction/transformation/re-articulation of identities that historically had been considered antagonistic to the popular project. In the particular case of the first years of the Sandinista Revolution, the figure of the landlord was hit hard by the new revolutionary laws because of the impact of what they were doing to both agricultural and urban property.[25] The popular project would find no place for this identity except in a form under which it had lost most of its economic significance. In 1984, it is the shopkeeper given to speculation who is most af-fected by the new mechanisms and regulations designed to ensure the supply of food and other goods to the population.

THE BOURGEOISIE

On the other hand, from the very beginning, revolutionary discourse has referred to the idea of a "patriotic bourgeoisie" as a fundamental element of the hegemonic system and of economic, political, and ideological pluralism. Regardless of the fact that members of the government may be of bourgeois origin and that they may even continue to enjoy the ownership and use of the means of production, the question is whether it will be possible to maintain the identity of the bourgeoisie as a class or whether the

24. On the question of worker participation in management, see CIERA, *ibid.*, pp. 100–23.

25. The National Reconstruction Government Junta fixed the maximum rent at a level several times lower than what was normal for the best land (300 cordobas per manzana for production of export crops and 100 cordobas for products destined for the domestic márket). See Decrees No. 230 and 263 (January 1980), *Leyes de la República.* Moreover, Decree No. 216 (December 29, 1979) reduced urban rents by up to 50 percent. Although these levels have not been maintained as a result of the incidence of market factors, the initial political–ideological effect has not been lost.

changes that it will have to undergo before becoming integrated into the hegemonic system will in effect lead to the dissolution of its class identity. The Sandinista project involves setting up a system of relations (identities) within which the private ownership of the means of production may be regulated by the profit motive in terms of particular decisions, while at the same time, when taken globally, remains subordinate to the satisfaction of the material and spiritual needs of the people and to the maintenance of popular sovereignty. In this context, the process of accumulation is regarded as a means rather than as an end. This is by no means impossible, particularly in view of the history of the Nicaraguan bourgeoisie. It could therefore reproduce itself as an economic class, putting forward its own particular demands on questions of public policy regarding the economy or labor relations, and so forth. However, in actuality, the popular hegemonic project, that is, the new system of social and political relations, would prevent the bourgeoisie from achieving its class project of imposing its own particular interests over those of the majority. It would thus be an "alienated" political class.[26] This would not prevent the bourgeoisie from participating in various government bodies, either as individuals or as representatives of a class organized corporatively or through the political parties. The pluralist project that is an integral part of popular hegemony makes it legally possible for the bourgeoisie to seek governmental power. However, the effective development and consolidation of popular power should be such that this objective cannot be achieved as a result of a stable correlation of forces that ensures that the majority's interests remain consensually dominant.

Theory tells us that, as it develops, capital invades every sphere of society, transforming all relations into mercantile ones and using the liberal state and parliamentary democracy as instruments of ideological and political domination over the masses,

---

26. On the "bourgeois question" in Nicaragua, see Chapter 2 of this book. One of the increasingly significant features of the relationship between the revolutionary government and the bourgeoisie is that the government maintains a continuous dialogue with and responds to demands from specific factions, but does not regard the associations that claim to speak on behalf of the class as a whole as valid spokesmen.

thus ensuring the atomization of the masses into individuals/ citizens. Nicaragua is responding to the challenge of arresting these global tendencies while ensuring the continued existence of private capital, albeit in a "deformed" state, as a result of its subordinate situation within the hegemonic system.

Another issue that must be raised and that also applies to the so-called noncapitalist middle sectors is the question of luxury spending. In a certain sense, the "realization" of much of the bourgeoisie in Nicaragua has been associated with the maintenance of privileged levels of consumption rather than with accumulation as such. This aspect of the bourgeoisie's identity should perhaps be controlled, in view of the need to further the general interest; however, a certain degree of inequality (not related to a project of domination) may be allowed.[27]

The Open Nature of the Hegemonic System

Several decades ago, we in Latin America learned that economic theories based on the notion of a closed economy were not applicable to our societies, showing as they do an exaggerated degree of openness and dependence on shifts in foreign markets and in the transnationals' power as well as on the economic policies of the center (as opposed to the periphery) states. However, openness and dependency also affect political systems. To think of hegemonic relations "as if" the national society was a closed system in which one can calculate correlations of forces on the basis of their social importance, their degree of organization, and the ideological relations among national social sectors, is to deny the reality of our societies.

The case of Nicaragua is obvious. Faced with the popular project expressed by the FSLN and the mass organizations, the na-

27. With this aspect as with many others, it is impossible to crystallize a revolution in accordance with a project "model." One of the results of the economic and military aggression of the Reagan administration, coupled with the crisis of world markets, has been to lead the government to introduce a program of macroeconomic adjustments that tends to drastically reduce luxury and nonbasic consumption, whereas the consumption of mass goods and salaries has been relatively less affected.

tional bourgeoisie had no opportunity to compete for a hegemonic role. With limited control over the mass media, with no possibility of obtaining support from the armed forces, lacking any strategy for economic development and for pulling the country out of the crisis other than continued dependence on the United States, the bourgeoisie was unable to offer a real political alternative. The two possibilities open to it were either to leave the country or to become actively incorporated into the "patriotic bourgeoisie" within the popular hegemonic system.

However, the Somocist system of domination was not a "national" system but a subsystem operating within a network of imperialist relations of domination that saw Central America as part of the United States' "backyard" and turned Somoza into their gendarme in the region. Moreover, defeating Somocism did not necessarily imply defeating imperialism. Once the battle was lost, the U.S. administration immediately began to lay economical and political seige to the revolutionary government, with the intention of influencing the definition of power in the country. Economic aid from the United States flowed toward sectors of the bourgeoisie and their allies in order to promote their activities and organizations. The aid ceased when the revolutionary government started to block these direct relations. The obvious consolidation of the popular forces in Nicaragua led American strategists to think that the only way to stop the revolution in its tracks was to reactivate the Somocist National Guard, which had already been expelled from the country. Washington set out to do this by organizing training camps first in Florida and later in Honduras with the support of the region's oligarchies. Finally, the aggression took the form of a relentless process of U.S. intervention in Nicaragua's internal affairs. It is difficult to say what the popular hegemonic project might have yielded under other conditions, but the fact is that imperialist initiatives helped to determine the subsequent development of events and to more clearly define the Nicaraguan people's anti-imperialist ideology.[28]

28. On the question of this identity that was forged during Sandino's struggle, see Sergio Ramirez, ed., *El pensamiento vivo de Sandino* (Managua: Editorial Nueva Nicaragua, 1984) and Carlos Fonseca, *Obras* (Managua: Editorial Nueva Nicaragua, 1982).

Parties and Movements: The Problem of Articulation

The social project emerging in Nicaragua is being developed on the basis of constructing an effective popular hegemony. The central elements of this project are the mass organizations and their dialectical relations with the FSLN and with the revolutionary government. These relations have been mediated by laws and institutions—which are often provisional—that have facilitated the regulation of conflicts, the establishment of instruments of participation, and the anticipation of the consequences of specific types of behaviors.

In 1984, Nicaragua was on the verge of taking an important step toward institutionalization by organizing elections to a National Assembly that would be made up of ninety representatives elected by district.[29] A law on political parties had already been approved. The electoral system would be based on universal suffrage, electoral competition among political parties, and pluralism through a system of proportional representation.

The question that arose was: How will the social movements be represented in these political structures? Or rather, what other structures should be created in order to ensure that some of these social forces will be able to participate in the political process at the level of the government? Then both political parties and social movements had been represented in the Council of State. By establishing suffrage as the instrument of representation, it no longer seemed possible to treat parties and movements within a common dimension, competing for social representation. This becomes obvious, not only because of the multiple identity of the social agents but also due to the need to maintain the specificity of movements and parties. The former are more oriented toward the expression of particular demands, whereas the latter have the function of synthesizing demands and integrating them into a

29. See the Law on Political Parties and the Election Law. This chapter was written before the Nicaraguan general elections held on November 4, 1984. The results of the elections to the National Assembly were as follows: FSLN, sixty-one seats; Democratic Conservatives, fourteen; Independent Liberals, nine; Social Christians, six; Communists, two; Socialists, two; and Marxist-Leninists, two. The FSLN obtained just under 67 percent of the vote in both the assembly and the presidential elections.

national project that, in turn, involves many dimensions that do not take the form of identities and of social movements.[30]

One possibility is that the political parties would include on their slate representatives of various mass organizations that in a system of proportional representation, involved a process of negotiating the order of names on the slate and the incorporation of the movements' demands into the party program. However, if the social movements and their leadership are transformed into "vote getters" for the political parties, there could be a tendency toward something that can be observed in its extreme form in the United States. A party can become overloaded with contradictions and particular interests that are translated into a "salad" of partial promises that, taken as a whole, not only fail to make up a proper national project but are also incompatible with each other and are not viable as a package, with the result that they tend to slow down social change rather than inject into the social situation the dynamism it requires.

On the other hand, although organizational autonomy of the social movements as the expression of certain social forces seems to be desirable in a participatory democracy, at the same time, given the open-ended nature of the process of construction/transformation of popular identities, it becomes difficult for these to crystallize in clearly defined qualitative and quantitative situations.

Another institutional alternative that might be considered is that of a second chamber of a consultative-deliberative character, where issues of national significance would be debated and where the principal social forces of the country could express their points of view. In any case, direct participation by the mass organizations in various decision-making bodies would not be incompatible with these new forms of government.

This problematic has other consequences. Within the frame-

30. This is not always clear. In other countries, social movements organized around issues such as peace, human rights, or natural resources transcend the level of specific demands and take on the role of critics of the course humanity has taken.

work of a pluralist system, the dialectical relationship between the revolutionary party and the mass organizations can take two forms: Either the party is maintained as a cadre party, made up of selected cadres who, in many cases, emerge from the mass organizations, or else it becomes transformed into a mass party. This has important implications for the question of the articulation of the people. The cadre party not only sets tactical and strategic goals but is also physically present in the leadership of the mass organizations through the process of incorporating the outstanding leaders who wish to become militants of the party. The mass organization is present among, and in symbiosis with, the masses, seeing and absorbing their contradictions and achievements, where the figure of the "representative of the people" doubly relates with the party and with its specific bases. We must then ask ourselves whether, against manualistic-oriented "common sense"—given a prolongation of imperialist pressure on Nicaraguan society—the first model, which could be represented in the form of a tree with the FSLN at the top and the mass organizations lower down— might not be more vulnerable than the second, which would allow direct horizontal contacts among the various social movements.[31]

As a final observation, it is possible that the Church, is a current and also an organization rather than a social movement standing "next to" all the others to be found at the base of the movements as well as among various levels of the leadership. In this sense, the FSLN and Christianity could converge (or compete) in the task of consolidating and giving form to the revolutionary subject of the new Nicaraguan society.

31. In fact, recent developments seem to indicate that, given the need to strengthen the internal front and the very dynamics of the electoral system, the FSLN might find itself closer and closer to the mass party model, even though the term *vanguard* may remain.

In a certain way, this implies a partial "internalization" of the confrontation of identities and particular interests within the revolutionary party. We should not confuse the cadre/mass opposition with the vanguard character of the party. A mass party can perfectly well play a vanguard role in relation to the social forces within the conscious process of building a new society.

Epilogue: Some Theoretical Questions Arising from Revolutionary Practice in Nicaragua

In the Introduction, we attempted to present a theoretical discussion of social movements based on developments in Europe. In the second part of this chapter, we discussed the experience of the Nicaraguan revolution from this perspective and in so doing, we pointed sometimes explicitly and sometimes only implicitly, to a number of limitations of the original conceptual framework. In what follows, we shall consider some of the theoretical issues raised by the Nicaraguan revolution that theories of social movements must take into account.

In the first place, the identities referred to in the conceptual framework cannot be viewed as "attributes" that permit us to classify (or organize) individuals into groups (social movements). It is much more productive to think of them as interpersonal or social relations. In addition, they must not be seen as oppressed or alienated "essences" that must be liberated but rather as situations constantly being transformed by the revolutionary process. Moreover, these identities are not given, either in an embryonic or in a fully developed form; indeed, new identities may emerge, and others may disappear as a result of the process.

Just as a correct theoretical outlook must move toward synthesizing and reconstructing the object, which in this case means that the concept to be determined is that of the people, this movement is incomplete unless it is coupled with the perception of a complex subject, incorporating contradictions and being brought together by an internal hegemonic system. The fact that the working classes make up a majority and/or represent a historical emancipatory project determines the class content of this system, and the people emerge as the revolutionary subject through a complex network of organizations and institutions. At the level of political practice, where the objective is not to wipe out all forms of power but rather to ensure that social power is exercised by the people, the movement toward synthesis referred to earlier correlates with the process of articulating the social movements in which the political parties have historically played a central role. In particular, in reflecting on the process of achieving a correlation of power

82

that would lead to a break with the structures that subjugate the people, we must reintroduce the role of the revolutionary party, not only because it articulates specific movements into a front of social forces but also because, in many cases, it is a product of these movements and the way they gain global political efficacy. This is no less true of situations that are as different from that of Nicaragua as the European societies, where political parties have not been divorced, either in the past or in the present, from the process of creating and giving substance to the social movements.

In that sense, the people are a historically determined category, changing in line with the structural development of society and with changing circumstances, which are not to be reduced to a predetermined class nor to a collection of universally determined identities. Its internal structure as a hegemonic system includes articulation between party(ies) and social movements and leaves no room for "choosing" between one form or another of collective action. The historicity and the conjunctural character of the movements (and identities) leave open the possibility that they might disappear, lose their effectiveness, or become rearticulated as a result of these same processes of transformation. Should this be the case, it becomes difficult to come to terms with the tendency that can be observed in certain authors to predict (or indeed wish) that the political party system will be replaced by the social movements. Nor can we uphold the idea that the former might provide favorable and exclusive access to democracy or might have a greater capacity for developing the people as a subject. It is far more useful to think in terms of a thesis that would propose that the presence of social movements on the political scene is indicative of a genuine critique of the parties' ability to provide a channel for the expression of contradictory social developments and that their actions will, of necessity, result in a transformation of this political system. In the context of an authentic social revolution, in a society where the civil sphere has another kind of density, these dialectical relations can take other forms that are also historically determined. We begin to see this when we raise the issue of moving from a cadre party to a mass party, as we move from a phase of organization and accumulation of forces against the dominant regime to a phase of building popular power in the presence of a revolutionary government.

83

Once it has been accepted that political parties must be incorporated into the analysis, we must particularly examine the form of articulation between parties and movements. Here we find a "verticalist" alternative that places the mass organizations in a subordinate position vis-à-vis the party(ies), even when they feed it ideas and information, and we have the alternative of a party that "horizontally" articulates various identities and their corresponding popular organizations.

The preceding discussion does not represent an attempt to innovate in the area of theories of social movements. However, I have tried to highlight certain aspects of the questions that have not received the attention they deserve in recent forums. I also believe that Nicaragua is a unique laboratory that might allow us to test whether certain propositions—sometimes extrapolated from other societies to Latin America rather precipitously—have universal applications, while still keeping in mind that this comparative analysis may also put into doubt the validity of certain academic views with regard to Europe itself.

Chapter 4

1984: Elections in Revolution

The Novelty of the Nicaraguan Elections

On November 4, 1984 (George Orwell's year!), a heartening political event took place in Nicaragua that was transcendent not only for the Nicaraguan people but for all Third World peoples fighting for their liberation. The Nicaraguan people freely voted and elected candidates to the offices of president, vice-president, and to the National Legislative and Constituent Assembly (Table I). In and of itself, the integrity of these elections is a historical novelty in Nicaragua and surpasses the standards to which we unfortunately are accustomed as regards many Latin American countries and the Third World in general. But this is not the main reason for their importance. This event was a step forward in the formation of a political system that aspires to innovate democracy by legitimizing—through effective electoral mechanisms—a social project that advocates radical changes favoring the popular masses in the economy and in the country's political and ideological structures.

The election of representatives is not the principal nor the only means of legitimizing a revolutionary program or government. However, once periodic elections are incorporated as a structural component of a political system, they will have profound consequences and will open up contradictions that we will try to highlight.

Table 1
Results of the Elections for President, Vice-president, and the National Constituent Assembly

| | President and Vice-president | | | | National Constituent Assembly | | | | |
| | | Percentages | | | | Percentages | | | |
	Absolute numbers	Regis-tered voters	Votes cast	Valid votes	Absolute numbers	Regis-tered voters	Votes cast	Valid votes
Voting Places[a]	3,876							
Registered citizens	1,551,597							
Votes cast	1,170,142	75.4			1,170,102	75.4		
Abstentions	381,455	24.6			381,495	24.6		
Valid votes	1,098,933	70.8			1,091,878	70.4		
Void votes	71,209	4.6	6.1		78,224	5.0	6.7	
FSLN	735,967	47.4	62.9	67.2	729,159	47.0	62.3	66.8
PCD	154,327	10.0	13.0	14.0	152,883	9.9	13.0	14.0
PLI	105,560	6.8	9.0	9.6	105,497	6.8	9.0	9.7
PPSC	61,199	3.9	5.2	5.6	61,525	4.0	5.3	5.6
PC de N	16,034	1.0	1.4	1.5	16,165	1.0	1.4	1.5
PSN	14,494	0.9	1.2	1.3	15,306	1.0	1.3	1.4
MAP–ML	11,352	0.7	1.0	1.0	11,343	0.7	1.0	1.0

Source: Supreme Electoral Council.

[a]There were a total of 3892 voting places in the country. Sixteen did not open due to the direct effects of the war.

The Election Results

It is very difficult to interpret the results of the election by means of a historical comparison using the "normal" methods applied to systems with a democratic tradition because these elections constitute a break with a regime characterized by fraud and corruption and by the complicity of those few invited to participate in order to legitimize the Somoza dictatorship. Therefore, it is irrelevant to compare these quantitative results with those of the previous elections. This is why observers have tended to analyze the percentages obtained by comparing them with the forecasts made by the participants themselves. The majority of the parties, including the FSLN that had constantly mentioned a margin of 80 percent of the vote, had no objective basis for their predictions because they did not have a history of organization and participation in previous elections. In fact, the large majority of the voters exercised this right for the first time in their lives, and several political parties (including, among others, the FSLN itself) had their first opportunity to compete for their share of the electorate.

The Political Content of the Elections and the Coordinadora Democrática

Elections are not held in a power vacuum. Some of the opposition candidates complained that, as the incumbent party, the FSLN had an advantage. But they did not mention the disadvantages caused by being in power during a period of such serious problems as foreign aggression, economic crisis, and being hampered by a legacy whose origins tend to disappear from the minds of a population facing the daily problems of survival. In any case, these elections were held within a framework defined by a revolutionary power that is confronting foreign enemies and difficulties derived from both the general international crisis and from the contradictions of the revolutionary process itself. However, in Nicaragua, the correlation of forces—which "domestically" would seem to have been strongly in favor of the FSLN in the preelection period—could not be measured merely in terms of the actions

87

of the political parties or of corporative organizations (business organizations and unions) and their respective social bases nor in terms of their ability to mobilize in the streets for or against production nor for or against defense.

In effect, a group of politicians calling itself the Coordinadora Democrática Ramiro Sacasa (Ramiro Sacasa Democratic Coordinating Group) was chosen by the Reagan administration to play a role within Nicaraguan society and the political system that was disproportionate to its social base. Its strength was supposed to be the reflection of the decision by the foremost world power—with its long history of hegemony and intervention in this region—that the Coordinadora was the only valid opposition force and the alternative to the revolutionary power. In order to support its "election," the Reagan administration used all of its national and international propaganda apparata and gave the Coordinadora Democrática the chance to speak in the name of the counterrevolution that is armed and run by the same administration. In addition, it treated it as its legitimate interlocutor, creating expectations that it could bring a much desired peace, presenting a political platform based on the promise of ending the armed struggle, the economic boycott, and the constant invasion threats. This was both its real and imagined strength—real because the material pressure exercised by the Reagan administration against the Sandinista People's Revolution cannot be denied; imagined because it could not meet the condition demanded by the most elementary democratic condition: that it base itself within the Nicaraguan people themselves. Internationally, the Reagan administration portrayed the Coordinadora as a giant, but in Nicaragua, this giant had clay feet.

Conscious of the Coordinadora's domestic weakness, the FSLN did all it could to have the Coordinadora participate on the national political scene. Equally aware of this same point, the Coordinadora decided not to run. The conversations held in Río de Janeiro in October in the presence of the Socialist International were the culmination of a series of concessions made regarding the schedule of the elections that had been sponsored by the FSLN so that the truly national forces could be measured. By then, the game being played by the Reagan administration had become so obvious that the other important international political groups had to openly criticize the Coordinadora's decision not to participate.

At the same time, the political forces willing to participate in the race had a national summit meeting, out of which emerged preelection accords regulating the strategic and not merely the tactical nature of the mechanisms and the conditions of representative democracy as the components of a political system in transition. Another accord was to call for a national dialogue in which "all the political, social, and economic forces in the country participate . . . in the effort that all Nicaraguans have the duty to undertake in favor of the nation's peace, stability, and progress," keeping the door open for the Coordinadora to at least participate in this part of the national political system (see Appendix).

The Meaning of the Election Results

When abstaining from the elections was the last resort open to the "principal opposition force" that claimed to have been marginalized from the political process, imperialism and its "representatives" were doubly defeated. On the one hand, 75.4 percent of the citizens chose to vote in order to express their party preference (the vote was not obligatory). On the other hand, the percentage of registered voters who did not vote could not be interpreted as a result of a particular political position in a country under war and with no relevant tradition in the area of elections. The Coordinadora was going to have to admit that it had not been marginalized from the political process because it participated in the national dialogue meetings that took place before and after the elections.

If for just a moment we think of the people as a complex subject that votes in elections in order to define not only party preferences but also to legitimize or discard a proposed political system, the decision was clear: The Nicaraguan people opted for a pluralist system formed of political parties competing for power through electoral consultations, under the hegemony of the revolutionary leadership of the FSLN. This in turn implies the deepening and development of the political, social, and economic transformations of Nicaraguan society and the rejection of the North American imposition of matrices within which the people must decide their destiny. Here the elections were not held United States style, on the basis of an accumulation of promises directed at the different

89

sectors conforming the electorate, nor was there much room for creating "images." The crude situation of a revolution assaulted by imperialism also put forth polarized options: Either the revolution would continue to be led by the FSLN in opposition to powerful outside forces, or the proposal of the administration to stop the revolution's taking place in its "backyard" would be accepted. To vote, even for the opposition parties, was to accept the revolutionary proposal of combining political pluralism with profound social changes.

The Construction and Maintenance of Revolutionary Hegemony

By facing other political organizations in the electoral contest, the FSLN, the revolutionary vanguard that led the Nicaraguan people to victory against the Somoza regime—the most loyal defender of the system of U.S. domination in the region—effectively admitted that it would not build and sustain its hegemony only on the basis of its political–military efficacy or on the moral and social validity of its political objectives. The people would have to approve and give their active consent to the revolutionary program and to its implementation by the vanguard party. This consensus would also be measured in a manner that assured not only its quality and intensity but also its quantitative predominance, not just through collective demonstrations—in political meetings, campaigns, and in production—but also in the closed voting booth. And in this area, the FSLN accepts the historical challenge planted by imperialism, which in the end is the agent and reproducer of the regimes of domination that predominate in the capitalist periphery when full-scale military dictatorships are not imposed. Strong military means will be put into play to continue to lay siege to the revolution and to divert its efforts away from the construction of a new economy and society, toward the defense against foreign aggression. Strong *political* means will be applied in order to isolate the revolution, to sabotage its economic relations, and to undermine international solidarity. But, in addition, the full efficiency of the ideological apparata will be applied—as has systematically been done until now—to distort the true nature of the revolution, to create

90

and destroy international images, and also to influence the consciousness of Nicaraguans themselves. All this takes place in the historical context of a country that has been held back by decades of dictatorship and dependence, trapped in a system of national and foreign social relations and a system of values that are fertile ground for destabilizing actions, confusion, and alienation.

A look at the electoral data points out, in effect, an uncontestable fact: The choice of one or another political option does not exclusively correspond to class background. Some lower income groups voted for the Conservative Democratic Party. And, even though conservative parties have at times won elections in countries on this continent, it is more difficult to admit the validity of this fact in the context of a revolution that presents the people with an effective option for breaking with the historical subordination to which they have been submitted. It is not sufficient, then, to assume that the workers' historical project is to see the poor as the first priority of governmental action. Traditions, clientism, and decades of alienation are not erased even with a revolution with the exceptional qualities of the Sandinista revolution. In the same way, the inevitable errors and poor practices of governmental agents weaken the support of those affected, and the option of voting for those who criticize the government becomes more a vote of censure than the real choice of another social project. Not only the recognition of, but the continual rectification of, errors and bureaucratic vices becomes an important condition of legitimacy. The submission of officials who represent the revolutionary state to popular criticism is turned into a system of regulation of state power by direct popular power. In this, the vision that the alienation of the people is a result of economic necessity would be insufficient to guide the ideological struggle. It is the political practice, the organized and increasingly autonomous participation of the masses that is the principal determining factor of the new consciousness being formed. Clear proof of this is the vote that supported the FSLN under very adverse economic conditions, under which many popular sectors have only partially experienced economic betterment in terms of their historical demands due to the conditions inherited from the dictatorship and the crisis, together with the aggression of which this society is victim.

91

The FSLN has already given hints of how it will face this new phase in the construction of revolutionary hegemony: It will continue consolidating the new political system in its formal and informal institutions. At the same time, it will work in two internal fronts: It will maintain continual dialogue with political and corporative leaders, made possible by the political will to support a project on anti-imperialist national unity, but this will not be its most important task. Its basic political task will be with the masses, where it will promote their organization, their participation in the revolutionary tasks, developing better social pedagogy that will tend to definitively overcome alienation in the state—people relationship, both through the actions taken by various bodies as well as the Sandinista People's Army in the organization of the struggle against the counterrevolution. The constitution of the people as the subject of the revolution, the articulation of the mass organizations with the revolutionary party, and the relationship of both with the state will now face new challenges.

National Unity as a Condition for the Continuity of the Revolutionary Process

The democratization and development of a society on self-determined bases is a revolutionary task that will require decades to complete. One necessary condition for this process to continue is the consolidation of revolutionary power. National unity, people's power, and economic viability are fundamental components of this consolidation. Political and ideological pluralism and its material foundations—the reproduction of the mixed economy—are simultaneously the objective and the condition of the revolution. They are the objective in that the democratization of an inherited society is proposed as an immediate task, simultaneous with that of social transformation. They are the condition in that the interventionist force can only be politically delegitimized and stopped with a broad anti-imperialist national front, with the revolutionary forces in the vanguard.

In fact, the revolution presents a watershed for determining the limits of this national unity. It is not a matter of excluding national ideological currents or certain social classes. The only determining factor is the position adopted vis-à-vis U.S. intervention and the Somocist counterrevolution. Those who know the history of relations between the Nicaraguan people, Somocism, and U.S. interventions know that talking about imperialism in Nicaragua is not an exercise in rhetoric but instead correctly connotes the type of relations that the United States has tried to maintain with the nations of this region. The Sandinista Revolution is a political break with the system of U.S. domination and its principal agent in the region—the Somoza regime. The U.S. government's reactions have only strengthened the revolution's anti-imperialist character.

On this basis, the participation of the Coordinadora within the project of national unity is practically impossible if it does not modify some of its positions, which have clearly been dictated from the perspective of the Reagan administration. The door will remain open, but it will be the Coordinadora itself that must make the decision.

The Material Basis of National Unity

The achievement of national unity requires conditions that are not only related to political will but also to this unity's very materiality. If internal, unresolvable antagonistic conflicts arise, unity could be broken on behalf of opportunistic or economically oriented positions. The government has stressed the need for the private sector to sustain or increase production; in turn, the private sector has demanded incentives and conditions for doing so. Negotiations are held and terms of an agreement are reached. This is what has been happening over the years, and without a doubt, it will continue to happen unless organized big business groups openly launch a boycott of production in order to destabilize the revolution. A similar negotiation process occurs under different political suppositions with the workers in the rural areas and in the cities.

But classes are reproduced not only as a result of the relation they have with the means of production but also as a result of their

93

chances to achieve certain levels and forms of consumption. In this area, the revolution faces the contradiction of having to sustain some forms of luxury spending by the medium strata and businessmen at the same time as it sustains and develops the means to satisfy the basic needs of the population in general. All this takes place in conditions marked by an extremely serious deterioration in the terms of trade and an aggression that forces the country to divert important resources to defense. In turn, this makes the maintenance of an investment rate that could create the basis for breaking with dependence impossible. The increase and diversification of domestic production and the achievement of a substantial increase in international aid are needed for overcoming these contradictions. The revolution's economic viability requires, then, the mobilization of national and foreign productive resources, while at the same time it is closely related to the maintenance of national unity.

An Organized Population: The Ultimate Guarantee of the Revolution

The material basis of national unity and consensus must be reinforced through an effective social pedagogy that clearly explains the causal relationships that exist between imperialism and aggression on the one hand and everyday problems on the other. Also needed is a continual struggle against bureaucracy and the bad practices of government agents, who must be submitted to direct criticism by the popular organizations and the social sectors affected—as well as that transmitted through their representatives. In synthesis, it demands a continual revolution in the state that is necessarily incomplete and the development of an efficient programming of resources and of economic policy.

The participation of various political currents on the national scene—effective pluralism—is an important condition for the Sandinista revolutionary project. However, facing the polarization continually being imposed by the situation of foreign aggression and the possibility of its further escalation, in the final analysis, political pluralism does not provide the guarantee by itself that the Nicaraguan people can continue their process of self-determination. The only guarantee is the organization of the population and the fulfillment of the Sandinista slogan that says, "The People, the Army, Unity: Guarantee of the Victory" or the one that says, "One Single Army."

In Nicaragua, the citizens are armed and willing to fight house by house and village by village to defend their land and to have the right to choose as a nation the type of society they want. The mass organizations, which in many cases are still weak and in a formative stage, are developing their capacity for autonomous participation. But there is still much to be done in this area. The contradiction between the urgent need for popular organization and the desire that this be autonomous has been generating a relationship between the FSLN and the mass organizations whose final character will be defined by the process itself, and not by proposals made beforehand.

The priorities of defense and basic economic necessities force the FSLN to maximize its mass mobilization abilities and to emphasize the organic links between the party and the popular organizations. In a parallel manner, these same pressures lead to the emphasis on party control over the state apparatus. The war facing Nicaragua, like any other war, demands a coherent leadership, in which military actions cannot be separated from the organization of basic economic tasks, the management of investments, and the control over imports.

People's power implies, then, the voluntary and decided organization of the masses in their articulation, with the goal of presenting a formidable barrier to the enemy under a common tactical and strategic leadership. Secondary contradictions of all types that confront the people must be subordinated to the immediate task of defending not one particular type of revolution but the very possibility of revolutionizing society. At the same time, the different organizations must be prepared and trained to act autonomously and from their own particular perspective, in the confrontations with the enemy on the military, social, and ideological battlegrounds.

95

The Vocation of Nonalignment

U.S. aggression has generated even more political contradictions. The Sandinista People's Revolution has sustained its nonalignment as a position before a bipolar world. But, confronted by the military aggression and by serious economic difficulties, it requires the aid and solidarity of other peoples. It has tried to diversify this aid and its international relations. However, due to the very effects of the East–West confrontation that the Reagan administration has promoted around the world, only the socialist countries are willing to consistently provide the weapons that are indispensable for defending the country. The diversification of economic relations that have been maintained and even developed during the years of the revolution cannot occur on the military front, not as the result of a conscious decision made by Nicaragua but due to the extremely effective blockade that the United States has imposed in this area within the Western world. Soldiers, militia members, and peasants harvesting with a rifle on their shoulders cannot ignore the fact that only the socialist countries are willing to give them the weapons they need to defend their lives against the ex-Somoza guardsmen. If nonalignment implies not being a satellite of either major power, it does not mean that the Nicaraguan people—although always maintaining their freedom of opinion—cannot recognize the difference between the support received from socialism and the constant aggression received from U.S. imperialism.

In other areas, even though international solidarity with Nicaragua continues and is a significant factor for contributing to the sustaining of its vocation of nonalignment, in the face of the boycott in the multilateral credit organizations only the socialist countries seem to be willing to offer the substantial long-term aid needed for necessary economic development. The Sandinista project is to reinsert the country in the international arena, maintaining equal economic relations with the developed capitalist world, the socialist world, and the Third World. But this vocation requires a positive and clear response from these parties.

The Revolutionary Forms

The fact that the revolutionary government decided to move forward with the electoral process and the development of the representative bodies, in the midst of the threats of a U.S. invasion and everyday actions by the counterrevolutionary forces that were seriously hampering production in some parts of the country, indicates the FSLN's political vocation. The view that this institutionalization of democracy is not a concession but rather a way to strengthen the revolution is in itself a central in-process definition of the FSLN's revolutionary project. For the FSLN, the representative forms are not by themselves guarantees of a substantive democracy but will necessarily need to be accompanied by an acceleration of the other forms of democratization and of the growing participation of the organized masses. The future constitution will lay out the institutional mechanism through which partisan representation will be articulated in the National Assembly with the representation of the people's specific interests, the forms in which the control of the executive bodies of the representative assembly will be combined with the direct control on the part of the mass organizations. The fact that the FSLN has incorporated representatives of the various mass organizations into its slate of candidates does not resolve, but rather shifts, this contradiction.

At the same time, these political forces will be accompanied by the continual development of the economic and social transformations necessary for modernizing the country, for reducing dependence, and for increasingly subordinating economic activity to the satisfaction of the population's basic needs and self-determination. In addition, they will be accompanied by a political pedagogy that will help overcome the political parties' traditional electoral behavior, creating a basis for serious dialogue about the national project. The people's direct control over the means of survival—the means of consumption and production as well as the weapons—will be stressed. The process of self-transformation of the different social classes will be accelerated in challenges that the nation will face in the coming years. The country's economic, social, and cultural integration will be deepened in the context of the revolutionary project.

The Challenges of the Sandinista People's Revolution

All this is seen in the framework of a political system that does not correspond to the usual problematic of socialist revolutions under imperialist attack. The traditional problematic of the relationship between the state, the party, and the mass organizations gains particular prospects in the case of the Nicaraguan revolution.

The existence of a pluralist system of political parties situated both to the right and the left of the FSLN, the participation of these parties in the government's legislative bodies, and the commitment to maintain and develop the conditions for effective political competition for the support of the population have strong implications. The relation between the state and the revolutionary party is redefined in this framework, even more so if the FSLN continues its policy of including members of other political parties in its cabinet. The problematic of the army's partisan character (see the Appendix) in the summit meeting of the political parties and the FSLN agreed that "all Nicaraguans . . . [may] opt for any responsibility with the armed forces, solely on the basis of military and patriotic qualifications." The appeal for popular consensus expressed in recurring votes implies that the various parties will maintain a permanent proselytizing activity with the popular sphere. This supposes the possibility—which actually already does exist in Nicaragua—of parallel mass organizations with different partisan leadership or that within every unified body competition determines who assumes the political leadership of each organization. The freedom of organization would favor the first alternative in the area of trade unions, although it was already agreed at the summit meeting that the community and neighborhood organizations "will have a social function and will not be partisan in nature," although they "will be formed on the basis of the voluntary and selective participation by the people." In all areas, tendencies will arise toward partisan competition, and although the FSLN may compete and win in all arenas of this political struggle, its challenge as the revolutionary vanguard will also be that of politicizing the population without posing this politicization solely as a partisan option, whereas the revolution should confront formidable tasks that make national self-determination and popular sovereignty more than partisan slogans.

Within this process of political competition, another fundamental choice comes into play. If the FSLN proposes to organize itself as the vanguard with a proven revolutionary cadre, its articulation with the mass organizations will have to take place at the highest levels. If, on the other hand, it adopts the form of a mass party, its presence and development will be accompanied by the growth of the organized masses themselves. In either case, but especially in regard to the latter, the question of democracy within the mass organizations and the party itself is posed strongly in this political context.

How does one confront all these challenges, which arise from the very nature of the revolutionary project of Sandinism? And, in particular, how is this done under conditions of an aggression that does not let up and that rather is extended into new areas and with renewed intensity?

For the peoples of Latin America, following this process closely will provide a limitless supply of knowledge. But the active solidarity with the Nicaraguan people is also a necessary commitment because it is essential to understand that if there exists a good possibility of a fourth, direct U.S. invasion, which periodically appears to be imminent, the disappearance—also temporary—of the signs of an imminent invasion will not by itself allow Nicaragua to carry out the normal political and social struggles of an institutionalized system. On the contrary, this new institutionalization is being painfully built in the context of a real war, unleashed in 1981 by the counterrevolutionary forces, that has caused more than 8000 deaths and that stretches to its limits the cohesion of a society that has proposed transforming itself in spite of its enemies. It is the responsibility of the entire continent, including U.S. citizens, to contribute so that Nicaragua can continue building new paths to democracy and socialism in Latin America. The principal contribution that this besieged people needs is peace.

Appendix

Summit Meeting of the Political Parties

In early October 1984, Nicaragua's political parties began a two-week summit meeting that included fifty hours of private meetings. The seven political parties registered for the November elections participated in the meeting: the Partido Popular Social Cristiano (PPSC—Popular Social Christian Party), the Partido Liberal Independiente (PLI—Independent Liberal Party), the Partido Conservador Demócrata (PCD—Democratic Conservative Party), the Frente Sandinista de Liberación Nacional (FSLN—Sandinista National Liberation Front), the Partido Socialista Nicaragüense (PSN—Nicaraguan Socialist Party), the Partido Comunista de Nicaragua (PC de N—Communist Party of Nicaragua), and the Movimiento de Acción Popular Marxist-Leninista (MAP-ML—Popular Action Movement [Marxist-Leninist]).

The summit meeting came about as the result of a series of meetings held by the six opposition parties—all the registered parties with the exception of the Sandinista Front. Following the failure of talks held in late September, these parties called for a national dialogue. The aim of such a dialogue would be the incorporation of the parties belonging to the Coordinadora, which were abstaining, into the November elections. The FSLN accepted the call for national dialogue.

The goal of the summit meeting was to gather the various Nicaraguan political parties' contributions to a dialogue that would end with a consensus on the framework for developing Nicaragua's economic and political systems. Although the parties belonging to the Coordinadora had long demanded a "national dialogue," they rejected the invitation to participate in the summit. Following long discussions about the economic, political, and electoral situation facing Nicaragua, a series of accords was drawn up during the summit that was signed by the seven parties. The accords dealt with a wide variety of topics, including civil liberties, the protection of private property, local elections, an apolitical armed forces, and the review of criminal cases.

Accords of the Meeting of the Registered Parties

Inspired by the feelings of patriotism, the parties, signed below, PPSC, MAP-ML, PCD, FSLN, PC de N, PLI, and PSN, have met during October and make the following announcement to the Nicaraguan people:

1. We have been brought together by the fact that during the dictatorship, we fought—although with different conceptions and methods—for a change that would bring liberty and justice to the Nicaraguan people.
   2. Recognizing the political and ideological differences that we have as parties, we are united by the patriotic responsibility of contributing to the search for peace, stability, and progress for our nation and our people.
   3. We were all brought together by the principle that Nicaragua's self-determination and sovereignty should be expressed in the response given to the problems presented by our country's stability and development. This response should be the sole domain of Nicaraguans, and it should be our people who determine the development of their political process without hoping for or accepting dictates from anyone.
   4. We were all brought together with the recognition that the aggression we now suffer threatens to reach levels that would dramatically affect every Nicaraguan and the Central American region's already troubled peace and stability.
   5. We have been brought together by the fact that, regardless of our programmatic differences, we consider it our duty to work toward creating the political, social, economic, and international

101

conditions that will neutralize these threats and contribute to obtaining peace for our people and the Central American region.

6. In regard to our respective political conceptions, we have all come to this meeting together with history and with our people, to establish the bases that guarantee the defense of our homeland, peace for Nicaragua, the democratization of the revolution, national development, and our people's welfare.

This desire is expressed in the following accords of political commitment and patriotic action:

A. To continue with the task of the democratic institutionalization of our revolutionary process, including:
   1. Periodic elections.
   2. Freedom of the press and the dissemination of ideas.
   3. The freedom to organize.
   4. Freedom of movement and travel.
   5. The right to organize and union democracy.
   6. All Nicaraguans, regardless of political and religious creed, shall have the right and duty to participate in the defense of the homeland and the revolutionary process and be able to opt for any responsibility within the armed forces solely on the basis of military and patriotic qualifications.
   7. Within the context of the mixed economy, the government will guarantee different forms of ownership, which include but are not restricted to the following: state, private, cooperative, and personal property as well as combinations thereof that are based on the rules and regulations that the laws establish in favor of the nation's interests.
   8. Once the Constitution of the Republic has been promulgated, elections will be held to democratically elect municipal authorities. Without disregarding the authority of the central government, they will enjoy sufficient freedom of action and will keep the local citizenry informed of their administrative activities.
   9. All community and neighborhood organizations will be formed on the basis of voluntary and selective participation by the people; they will have a social function and will not be partisan in nature.

B. To maintain and broaden the democratic freedoms that the revolutionary process has already achieved.
   1. All political parties registered for the elections will keep their legal status regardless of the outcome of the vote.
   2. The political parties registered and participating in the current electoral campaign will maintain the right to use the state-owned media throughout the constituent period, in proportion to their share of the vote.
C. We agree to the following in order to better conditions for the current electoral campaign:
   1. Make a general call to the members and sympathizers of the different political parties to put an end to mutual harassment of any kind that obstructs the electoral race, especially regarding the taking of reprisals and coercion. The new government shall also guarantee that no repressive measures will be taken against the members and sympathizers of the political parties as a result of their campaign activities and will guarantee their jobs in autonomous state or private enterprises. Nor will discriminatory commercial or other measures be taken that would violate citizens' rights.
   2. Activities will be undertaken to reform the existing Electoral Law, so that the voter's Civic Card will be handed in upon casting a vote and can be reclaimed once a reasonable period of time has elapsed, that shall be no less than two weeks.
   3. A commission formed of members of the registered parties will jointly name the third member of each voting board.
   4. Through the UPN (Nicaraguan Union of Journalists), new programming will be begun on state-owned radio and television stations to allow the registered political parties to increase their political propaganda.
   5. Arrangements will be made to extend the electoral campaign to include the twenty-four hours of November 2.
   6. As part of the reforms made to the Electoral Law, leave without pay will be extended until November 19. For purposes of determining salary, the average salary earned the last six months before the granting of the leave will be used as reference.

7. All the political parties together reaffirmed their condemnation of the aggression the country is presently suffering.

D. In hopes of perfecting the application of justice, we have decided:

1. The representatives of our political parties who are elected to the National Assembly will take on as prioritized tasks, among others, the revision of the application of the right to habeas corpus and the streamlining of judicial procedures to allow a more effective application of justice.

   This Commission will also immediately begin to examine the cases of those sentenced by the Special Tribunals and the Popular Anti-Somocist Tribunals, who have lesser sentences or due to humanitarian reasons or good conduct, could be favored with a pardon.

2. The National Assembly should examine the problematic of implementing the right to legal defense because it presents complex factors and it is necessary to deepen its study.

E. In order to assure the realization of these efforts toward peace, we have decided:

1. The political organizations participating in the present electoral campaign commit themselves to immediately put all possible accords into practice and to reflect them in a concrete way in the Constitution of the Republic through their future representatives in the National Assembly.

2. In agreement with the goals defined in the call made to this Summit Meeting of the Political Parties, we agree to call on all the political, social, and economic forces in the country to participate in a national dialogue and to participate in the effort that all Nicaraguans have the duty to undertake in favor of the nation's peace, stability, and progress.

3. We approve the formation of a special committee formed of representatives of the political parties designed . . . to guarantee and provide follow-up on the implementation of these accords.

   Said committee will take charge of carrying out the necessary consultations for organizing the national dialogue.

Index

Accumulation model, ix
Agrarian reform, x–xi, 29
Agriculture, 3
AMNLAE (Luisa Amanda Espinoza Nicaraguan Women's Association, 63, 69
AMPRONAC (Association of Women Concerned about the National Problematic), 62
APP (People's Property), 74
Association of Women Concerned about the National Problematic (AMPRONAC), 62
Autonomy Project, xii

"Basic Statute," 49
Bourgeois question, 13, 45–47
Bourgeoisie, 3, 75–77
  cotton, 46n

Cadre party, 81, 83
Campaign, electoral, 103–104
Catholic Church, 70–71, 81

CAUS (Confederation for Union Action and Unity), 6
CDS (Sandinista Defense Committees), xi, 29, 37, 48, 62–63, 67
Censorship, 28–29
Central American Common Market, 3
Christianity, 2
Church, Catholic, 70–71, 81
Class struggle, 73
Classes, working, 72–75, 82
Confederation for Union Action and Unity (CAUS), 6
Conjunctural situation, 69
Constitution, x
Contadora Group, xiii, xv, 4
Coordinadora (Ramiro Sacasa Democratic Coordinating Group), 88
COSEP (High Council of Foreign Enterprise), 6
Costa Rica, xv
Cotton bourgeoisie, 46n
Council of State, 79
CRIES (Regional Coordinating Board of Economic and Social Investigation), xvi

meaning of, 9–10
of representatives, 42
Liberation Front, National, *see*
    Sandinista National
    Liberation Front
Luisa Amanda Espinoza
    Nicaraguan Women's
    Association (AMNLAE), 63, 69

Managua, viii
Mass organizations, 43
Massification, 21
Media, 44
Military draft, vii, ix
Minorities, ethnic, 71–72
Miskito question, xi–xii
MISURASATA, 37, 71
Municipal government, 67–69

National Assembly, x, 49–50
National Farmers and
    Cattlemen's Union (UNAG),
    29, 37, 68
National Liberation Front, *see*
    Sandinista National
    Liberation Front
National Literacy Campaign, 4
National question, 44–45
National Reconstruction
    government, 36
National unity, 5–6, 25
    material basis of, 93–94
    revolution and, 92–93
Nicaragua, *see* National *entries*,
    Sandinista *entries*
Nonalignment, vocation of, 96

Parties
    cadre, 81, 83
    political, *see* Political parties

Patriotic Military Service, vii
Peasants, 66–67
"People," concept of, 58–59
People's power, 95
People's Property (APP), 74
People's Revolution, *see*
    Sandinista People's
    Revolution
Pluralism
    effective, 94–95
    political, 8
    within revolution, 26–28
Pluralist system, 7
Political content of elections,
    87–89
Political organizations, 43
Political parties, 79–81, 84
    summit meeting of, *see*
    Summit meeting of political
    parties
Political Parties Law, 50
Political pluralism, 8
Political power, 16
Politics, economics and, 16
Popular power, 35
Power, 15–16
    forms of, 17–22
    people's, 95
    popular, 35
Power relations, 60
Proletarianization, 39–40
Proletariat, 12
    dictatorship of, 23
    role of, 38–40

Ramiro Sacasa Democratic
    Coordinating Group
    (Coordinadora), 88
Reagan, President Ronald,
    52–53; *see also* United
    States

For Product Safety Concerns and Information please contact our EU
representative GPSR@taylorandfrancis.com
Taylor & Francis Verlag GmbH, Kaufingerstraße 24, 80331 München, Germany

www.ingramcontent.com/pod-product-compliance
Lightning Source LLC
Chambersburg PA
CBHW071135280326
41935CB00010B/1242

9 7 8 1 0 3 2 7 8 3 5 7 4